OUTWITTING

SQUIRRELS

101 Cunning Stratagems to Reduce
Dramatically the Egregious
Misappropriation of Seed From Your
Birdfeeder By Squirrels

 Bill Adler, Jr.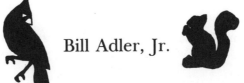

Chicago Review Press

To my parents, who I constantly tried to outwit as a child, and who, sometimes, lovingly let me get away with it.

Library of Congress Cataloging-in-Publication Data

Adler, Bill.
    Outwitting squirrels.

    1. Bird feeders. 2. Squirrels—Control.
3. Squirrels—Humor. 4. Mammals—Control.
5. Mammals—Humor. I. Title.
QL676.5.A34   1988   639.9′78   88-20283
ISBN 1-55652-036-0 (pbk.)

Published by Chicago Review Press, Incorporated,
814 N. Franklin Street, Chicago, Illinois, 60610

CONTENTS

Acknowledgments

The perennial fear among writers with acknowledgments is that you're going to leave someone out. With a book like *Outwitting Squirrels: 101 Cunning Stratagems to Reduce Dramatically the Egregious Misappropriation of Seed from Your Birdfeeder by Squirrels*, however, the danger is just the opposite: I might mention somebody who's too embarrassed to be associated with this book.

Still, I couldn't have done it alone. My thanks go first to squirrels who volunteered to let me test the squirrel-proofness of various feeders on them. Second, I want to thank the hundreds of birds who patiently waited out these squirrels, while the squirrels prevented them from getting to the seed.

A number of humans also gave invaluable assistance. I want to thank Peggy Robin, who let me use her back yard as a proving ground for feeders. Peggy's criticisms and suggestions when *Outwitting Squirrels* was still tucked inside my wordprocessor helped make this a better book.

George Petrides, proprietor of The Wild Bird Center, was a fountain of information about birds, squirrels and people who feed both. As I was interviewing people for this book, nearly everyone said I have to talk to Professor Vaun Flyger, one of the country's foremost squirrel experts. I did, and I appreciate his lending me his knowledge for *Outwitting Squirrels*. Heidi Hughes, who owns The Wild Bird Company, had many valuable things to say about feeding birds, especially about keeping birds safe from human-inspired hazards. Liz Cummings at the U.S. Fish and Wildlife Service offered numerous perspectives into the personalities of particular species.

Richard Mallory, publisher and editor of the *Dick E. Bird News,* graciously allowed me to reprint articles and illustrations from his wonderful newspaper. His insight into squirrels and birds was a valuable resources.

A number of wild bird product companies and distributors graciously offered me their years of experience in dealing with squirrels. I want to thank Marlene Couter of Duncraft, Olin Looker of Looker Products, Dr. Stephen Clarke of Clarke Products, Thomas Post of The Audubon Workshop, Richard Clarke of The Bird House, and Marie Gellerstedt of Nixalite of America.

Dekun Photo processed and printed most of the photographs in *Outwitting Squirrels.*

My thanks also go to Richard Swain for letting me republish his essay, "The Squirrel and the Fruitcake," here.

My friend and neighbor Stephanie Faul originally got me interested in feeding birds several years ago. She had no idea it would lead to this.

It's hard to write a book as fun and informative as *Outwitting Squirrels* without wanting to read sections to people as you go along. Several friends graciously listened to paragraph after paragraph—not all polished at the time—as I progressed. (All I had to do was promise not to write *Outwitting Squirrels II.*) These friends include, Marta Vogel, Mitch Schultz, and Carol Dana.

And of course, this book never would have been published if it weren't for Linda Matthews of Chicago Review Press, who was willing to risk having an entire species vow never to use Chicago Review Press as their publishers. This book benefited greatly from Linda's suggestions and experience.

Introduction

"They're here." That may be a line from the movie Poltergeist, but it's also the horror-cry of the tens of millions of Americans who feed birds, as they prepare to fend their feeders from hordes of squirrels. Each day, tons of birdseed is poured into birdfeeders to attract and benefit beautiful, winged creatures—cardinals, doves, chickadees, goldfinches—and each day, tons of birdseed is pilfered by marauding squirrels. If there's one thing that birders have in common it is their common enemy: the squirrel.

Mention squirrels to any bird feeder and you will inspire a half-hour monologue about how these cunning little mammals managed to overcome the most inventive, dangerous-looking, and expensive anti-squirrel systems. Sometimes you have to believe that if the creativity and energy that bird feeders put into thwarting squirrels were directed toward world peace or eliminating traffic jams we'd have no more earthly problems.

People who feed birds have tried every possible anti-squirrel concoction their imaginations can conjure. Every situation seems to demand its own "solution." Defensive options range from water cannons to giving squirrels feeders of their own. From barbed wire and electrified feeders, to coating birdfeeders with Ben Gay and teflon, to baffling the top and bottom side of feeders so that birds can barely get in—nothing seems to work.

Until now. Until *Outwitting Squirrels: 101 Cunning Stratagems to Reduce Dramatically the Egregious Misappropriation of Seed From Your Birdfeeder by Squirrels.* For the first time, the sum of humankind's knowledge about squirrels and how to defeat them is available in one place.

Writing *Outwitting Squirrels* was one of the most pleasurable experiences I've had as an author. There are few topics that lend themselves to both a serious examination and playfulness. While researching *Outwitting Squirrels* I talked with dozens of people in the bird business and with ordinary birders with extraordinary squirrel problems. I was impressed by the inventiveness and persistence of the bird feeders who tried to keep squirrels at bay— and impressed by the squirrels. I was entertained by people's stories about squirrels. I believe that reading *Outwitting Squirrels* will be as much fun for you to read as writing it was for me.

Who are we, the people who feed wild birds and scream and flail our arms at squirrels? Where do we fit in the range of what "normal" Americans do? You'll be pleased to know that bird-feeding and squirrel yelling are common practices. We bird feeders participate in the second most popular hobby in America, after gardening: there are eighty million Americans who dish out meals to birds. We spend over $500 million a year on birdseed, $54 million on birdfeeders, $25 million on birdbaths, and $17 million a year on bird books. There's a tremendous amount of interest and money involved with feeding birds. And wherever there are birdfeeders, there are squirrels.

As annoying and frustrating as squirrels are, they are humorous as well. After all, squirrels think that the birdseed is for them and there's no power on earth that will convince them otherwise.

So while *Outwitting Squirrels: 101 Cunning Stratagems to Reduce Dramatically the Egregious Misappropriation of Seed from your Bird- feeder by Squirrels* gives concrete, useful information that birders can use to stop squirrels from poaching, it's also a funny and philosophical book. Funny, because every time a human constructs another barrier, squirrels break through. Funny, also, because bird feeders spend hundreds of hours and dollars trying to keep these small animals away—and the squirrels have nothing better to all day long than break into feeders. Philosophical because there must be some overall significance to this human-bird-squirrel triangle. Right?

Maybe there's a meaning to these anti-squirrel antics, and maybe not. But there is one essential fact to keep in mind when it comes to squirrels: we are smarter and stronger than squirrels. We can win against squirrels. We will win against squirrels. And along the way, we're going to have plenty of fun.

1

Misadventures With Squirrels

"I'm getting low on bird food and I don't know what the squirrels will do without my bird feeder to raid."

Sandy Rovner, *Washington Post*

It could happen to anyone. Of that I'm now sure. And it could happen to anyone in the most innocent, innocuous way. Oh, yes, I know, because it happened to me. Once I was like most people, caring, tolerant, even curious of the natural world, but that is a distant part of my past now. I really can't remember what I used to be like—before. I can only hope that by writing this chapter I can warn others before they, too, are obsessed, are controlled by a single, overriding hatred—of squirrels (at least when they come in proximity to birdfeeders.)

My apartment building doesn't allow pets. (Except for "grandfathered" pets, those that were here before this rule was instituted. It was my lot to live in the apartment below Dusty, a four-legged tap-dancing dog, who likes to wake his owner by practicing his Fred Astaire routine at 6 A.M.) I never actually wanted a cat or a dog, figuring that owning one would be a reasonably large hassle for an apartment dweller, but as soon as I learned of this no-pets rule, I decided I needed one.

When I visited a friend's apartment and saw a birdfeeder attached to her window, surrounded by all sorts of colorful and (to my eye) exotic birds, I knew that's what I had to have. A feeder would be perfect—I would not have just one pet, but dozens. I wouldn't have to walk them, change their litter box, or vacuum my clothing every morning. Most important, I could have these pets and not get evicted. My friend gave me her Duncraft bird catalog, and through the miracles of modern credit, my feeder arrived in less than a week.

I opened the box quickly, followed the instructions carefully (soak the two suction cups in warm water for 3 minutes, then rub them with your finger to increase their sticking power), added a quart of Safeway wild bird food mix from the 10 pound supply I had already purchased in anticipation, slapped the feeder on the window, and waited. It was five in the afternoon in February. I kept waiting for my birds to arrive.

Nobody told me that birds don't come to feeders after dark.

But the next day was amazing. My feeder brought a sunset-red cardinal, two doves, a couple of finches, a chickadee, a tufted titmouse, a warbler, a junco, and a white-breasted nuthatch. (I know this because I also bought the *Audubon Society Field Guide to North American Birds*.) I'd never seen anything like this before— beautiful birds with beautiful songs coming to my window every handful of seconds. I'd just sit at my desk and look at them, or sometimes I'd walk over to the window for a closer view. A few birds like the tufted titmouse and the chickadee didn't mind my standing so close to them; others would fly back to the nearby tree and wait for my departure. It didn't bother me that some of these birds wouldn't let me come close; after all, they provided so much enjoyment and required so little in return—just sunflower seeds. On the rare occasion when a minute or two passed without a bird stopping by, I'd become terribly disappointed.

One afternoon something happened that changed my world forever. It inspired a quest that has been driving me for nearly two years; the same quest that motivates 80 million other Americans. That February afternoon, I returned from an errand, opened my door, and saw a squirrel in my feeder. My birdfeeder! The whole squirrel—tail and everything—was inside the feeder, a rectangular lucite compartment attached to my window with suction cups.

Nothing has been the same since.

For the rest of the afternoon I stood guard over the feeder, protecting my birds from this gray rodent. Every time it approached, I flailed my arms, banged on the window—and the squirrel ran away. Unfortunately, it didn't take too many hours before the squirrel learned that the window was solid, and despite my gestures and noise, I remained safely inside.

The squirrel, being a city creature and all, decided that it could stand the noise as long as it could eat. Sort of like dining at an outdoor cafe along a major street.

So I urgently developed a new strategy: I opened the window and yelled at the squirrel, who, recognizing the implications of an open window, bolted away. He returned; I opened the window. Now mind you, this was still winter, so I wasn't too crazy about opening my window every fifteen minutes or so to shake my fist at the squirrel, but what choice did I have? Anyway, the technique worked. This squirrel, which somehow managed to climb up two flights to my apartment, was defeated. I was victorious.

I was wrong.

The next morning it was back. Not only was it back, but the squirrel brought a friend. Still worse, my birds weren't around, apparently figuring that they ought to yield right-of-way to the gray animal with claws. But a squirrel's only a dumb animal, I thought, and it would only take a modicum of ingenuity and effort to thwart the squirrel's invasion. So I moved the feeder to a higher pane on my window, a couple of feet above the air conditioner. Sanguine over my success, I left the apartment for lunch.

When I returned, I discovered that I wasn't the only one who had been dining. Leaping a half dozen more inches from the air conditioner had posed no problem for the squirrel; in fact, he appeared to enjoy this spate of pre-lunch exercise.

All right, I thought, I'll let the squirrel get into the feeder, but for one purpose only: to watch how and from exactly what spot on the air conditioner he leaps. If I could learn the squirrel's technique, I knew that I could develop a counter to it.

This was the beginning of war.

In the meantime, I wasn't going to sit back and do nothing; my birds were counting on me. A trip to the hardware store would produce some useful ideas, I thought. I was right: at the store I found an item that I was certain would mean the squirrel's downfall, something that despite the squirrel's long lineage, extending back through generations of birdfeeder raiders, he wouldn't be able to overcome.

Before I tell you what that item was, I need to mention one other aspect of the squirrel's behavior. I noticed early on that Mr. Squirrel was adept at climbing brick walls. Very adept. In fact, it was the brick wall that the squirrel needed in order to invade my feeder. The wall was its attack route; a kind of Normandy beach of the squirrel world. Obviously, I couldn't remove the brick wall, but I could do something even better, thanks to a miracle-product of the 1980s: spray-can teflon.

With the glee of a sixteen-year-old on prom night, I coated the walls around and below the air conditioner with a visible film of teflon. Although I had to lean out the window precariously in order to reach every spot, it was worth the risk.

And I wasn't disappointed. The first squirrel that leapt onto the teflon-coated brick was as surprised as I was overjoyed: the moment his claws caught the teflon-coated surface he scrambled furiously to keep hold, his little legs moving rapidly in circles, as if he was being chased by a cat. It was a fun, funny, fantastic sight: here was Mr. Squirrel, so certain that he could scale any surface (except glass, but he already knew about that), but especially brick; and now ordinary brick was refusing to cooperate. The squirrel's world turned topsy-turvy; the squirrel had no basis on which to compare or comprehend this new reality created by teflon. From this moment on, there would be no rules that Mr. Squirrel could depend on.

Finally, teflon had a valuable application.

As you can tell, that wasn't the end of the war between me and the squirrels. Teflon was great while it lasted, but unfortunately spray teflon has one negative property: it comes off brick when it rains. Another alternative was brewing in my mind—spraying the squirrel with teflon—but I wasn't ready for anything like that. Yet.

Okay. I can live with a temporary setback, I said to myself: I have more tricks up my sleeve. If only I could think of them.

Frequently, the best inventions stem not from trips to the hardware store or Rube Goldberg contraptions that are the product of weeks of imagining. Rather, they result from making use of what's around you. The common, uncomplicated things. And that's precisely what I did.

Anyone who works in his apartment can tell you that there's a grave danger lurking for those who spend the day in this environment: the refrigerator. The refrigerator is the ultimate seductress for the work-at-home crowd; it is the force that moves waist size to increase faster than age. Not wanting to impersonate the individual who's girth determines that of the golden arches at McDonald's, I opted to stock my fridge with Perrier water, a nice, non-caloric alternative. But all those empty bottles! What a pain to throw away!

Yes, indeed—all those empty bottles provided the means to thwart Mr. Squirrel's birdfeeder rampages. You see, in order to jump into the feeder on the window, the squirrel had to leap from the top of my air conditioner. And he couldn't jump from just anywhere on the air conditioner: the angle had to be just right for him to get into the feeder. I'm a two-liter a day Perrier drinker; it took only a couple of days for me cover the squirrel's launch sites.

I could relax again.

My relaxation lasted exactly twenty-four hours.

The squirrel found new launch sites.

So I found new places to put Perrier bottles.

And then the squirrel started knocking the Perrier bottles down. I filled them with tap water to make them too heavy to knock down. Then the squirrel started bowling: he discovered that if you could knock down one Perrier bottle you could cause most of them to fall. That apparently was not only easier from the squirrel's perspective, but more enjoyable as well. My countermove was to encircle the bottles with copper bell wire to create a single, Perrier superstructure, too heavy for the squirrel to knock over.

Victory at last!

Wrong again. The squirrel decided to ignore the Perrier apparatus altogether and simply hoist himself up to the feeder by grabbing onto the wooden window frame and pulling himself upward, as if doing a chin-up. Mr. Squirrel even found that he could use the Perrier bottles as a support to balance his back legs against, as he lifted himself into the feeder.

My riposte was to spray the window frame with teflon, even though I knew it would only last until the next rain. Alas, I also sprayed the window with teflon, which made it difficult to see through.

Maybe I'm going about this all wrong, I figured. Perhaps the solution lies not in preventing access to the feeder, but in the type of feeder I have. Looking at the feeder, with its wide entry area and well defined edges—great for holding on to—I understood that I'd been making things too easy for Mr. Squirrel. It was time to play hardball.

I bought a new feeder—a chalet-style apparatus made of pine, with Plexiglas windows along the long sides. The seed was dispensed from a gap between the Plexiglas sides and wooden base of the feeder. In order to eat the feed, a bird (hopefully, only a bird) had to reach that narrow opening. By putting the feeder on top of the Perrier bottles there would be no way for the squirrel to get its furry little face into that opening; the space was simply too high and far away.

Again, I was simply wrong. I learned something new about squirrels' capabilities: they can, and will, eat through anything to get to food. In a few days the squirrel had eaten through the feeder to create a reasonable-sized hole through which he could munch to his stomach's content.

Enough! It has to be possible for a human to outwit a squirrel! Feeding birds was important, certainly; being surrounded by cardinals and titmice all day long is rather pleasant. No squirrel is going to stand in my way, I shouted silently. This was becoming more than a matter of being close to birds. Pride and intelligence were involved and I wasn't about the let a mere rodent get the better of me.

It's at this point in the story about my war with the squirrels that I'd like to digress. My Squirrel War was causing personal problems as well. Frequently while talking on the telephone, I would shout in the squirrel's direction: "Get out of here!" followed by certain epithets. My friends, of course, thought it rather rude that I would hurl insults at them without provocation. When I told them about the squirrel, that increased their concern for my mental health. So be it—I was not going to succumb to the squirrel's strategy.

I bought yet another feeder, a clear Swiss chalet-style feeder that attaches with suction cups to the window and has a wide opening in front. (Buying new feeders was to be a recurring phenomenon, part of the squirrel's strategy, I'm certain. If he couldn't win by being more patient and persistent than me, he was going to make me very, very poor. Of course, he probably didn't realize that if I could no longer afford new feeders, I couldn't afford more feed.) Attaching a feeder directly to the window was a return to the old, unsuccessful geometry, I knew, but the height of the feeder on the window pane was an advantage; I intended to take that advantage. This feeder's opening was in the front, with suction cups on the back. Fortunately, the opening of this feeder was arranged so that the squirrel couldn't leap directly in. But I knew that if I simply attached the feeder to the window, the squirrel would be able to leap on top of it and crawl inside. The Swiss chalet had a very steep roof, and it was this fact that I intended to exploit. Because of its steepness and because the chalet was constructed of lucite, the squirrel would have a difficult time securing himself to the top so as not to fall. (I had discovered by this time that squirrels aren't afraid of heights, falling, losing their balance or anything like that at all; but they can fall.) When on the chalet the squirrel would have to devote some of his claws to supporting himself while he climbed over the top into the feeder—the only way to the food. Knowledge is the human species' most powerful tool. By pressing this knowledge to its outer edge I was certain I could win. Carefully, I drilled holes spaced about 1/4 inch apart in the feeder's roof, near the front edge. I then placed 3 inch nails, pointing upward, in these holes, creating a barrier to prevent the squirrel from leaning over the edge of the roof and climbing into the feeder from the top. I also placed a couple of upward-pointing nails on the feeder to make it more difficult for the squirrel to meander around the top. These nails were positioned more or less in the center of the upside down V-shaped roof top. The feeder looked intimidating: kind of medieval, frightful. Sometimes I could see the sun reflect off the nails' points; and suddenly I felt as if my feeder-fortress had a consciousness—it knew its purpose. In a strange way, it was an evil creation designed to inflict good.

And here's what happened. First, the squirrel used the nails as hand-holds—he wrapped one claw around a nail. Second, by some ability I am at a loss to describe, Mr. Squirrel simply passed through my wall of nails as if they weren't there. Because the nails were pointing up along a triangular surface, geometry forced the space between the nails to get larger the farther the nail was from the surface of the feeder. Yet somehow the squirrel lifted himself into the air and pushed through the open part. I countered by weaving copper wire between the nails to fill that space; it looked like a fence. Now the squirrel had to scale the fence, and flip upside down to get inside the feeder. He did.

It was time for heavy artillery. I bought a squirt gun and blasted the squirrel every time he came near the feeder. Naturally, this meant that I didn't get much work accomplished, but so what? War requires sacrifice. Although Mr. Squirrel wasn't too crazy about me, after a while he didn't seem to care about being sprayed with water. It didn't take long for the squirrel to figure out that what I was squirting him with was the same stuff that falls from the sky. So I escalated and bought a dart gun—the kind with the red, rubber tips so I wouldn't actually harm the squirrel. (While bird feeders may hate squirrels, we are, deep down, nature lovers.) And I got pretty good—I could hit a moving squirrel at 20 feet. My objective with the dart gun was to annoy the squirrel enough so that he'd move elsewhere—to somebody else's feeder. While I did annoy him (though when the dart hit the squirrel at its maximum range, 20 feet, the impact was so soft that the squirrel just shook itself and went back to whatever it was doing) the squirrel developed a countertactic: eat while I wasn't watching. He knew that by the time I grabbed my gun, reached the window and opened the screen, he would be well out of range. In response I would sometimes lie in wait with dart gun in hand—ambush style—beneath my window and spring to fire while the squirrel wasn't looking. Ultimately, however, I tired of this faster than the squirrel did.

It was then that I read about Nixalite in an article in the *New York Times*. Nixalite's another product of the technology of the miraculous 1980s, like teflon, I guess: only better! The article in the *Times* discussed how effective Nixalite was at keeping pigeons from roosting on building ledges. It was particularly helpful to owners of historical properties, who prefer not to have their architectural masterpieces covered with pigeon droppings. (I guess it's fair to malign pigeons in a book that's pro-bird; they're not really birds, but are more akin to, as Woody Allen once said, "rats with wings.") Nixalite is a prickly, barbed-wire type of material; it comes in 12-inch strips, with sharp three-inch spines protruding out of the strip. The spines all extend in the same direction, but at varying angles, making it impossible for a pigeon to alight on them. Nixalite can be handled from the bottom, but you definitely wouldn't want to grab it from the sharp side. Presumably, a squirrel wouldn't want to leap onto that side, either.

If you were a squirrel, would you get close to Nixalite?

I bought yet another feeder, a new wood and Plexiglas chalet-feeder (the same kind I'd had before). I placed the Nixalite around the tops of the Perrier bottles so that the squirrels couldn't chomp away at my feeder. This time I was certain that the squirrels wouldn't be able to get into the feed and that—soon—they would become frustrated and go away. My feeder was surreal and scary. There it was, with sharp spines protruding in all directions. A danger. H.P. Lovecraft would be proud. *I* wouldn't want to try to get into the feeder.

But I'm not a squirrel. Mr. Squirrel was undaunted by the Nixalite. At first he tried to eat it. (I've discovered that metal is just about the only thing squirrels can't gnaw through). Instead of giving up (something I've also discovered isn't a squirrel in-stinct), he just leapt to the top of my alpine-shaped feeder and fed himself upside down.

Attack, retreat, then counterattack. This was truly war and I was not about to lose!

To prevent the squirrel from using the top of the feeder as a hanging-off-point, I placed the terrifying-looking Nixalite spines on the top of the feeder. Satisfied, I went back to work.

By this time, Nixalite covered the feeder. It was impenetrable, with openings available only to creatures that fly. But again, I underestimated the depth of Mr. Squirrel's determination. At first he began to eat through the sides of the wooden feeder; and as he was close to achieving success, abruptly changed his strategy and decided simply to push the Nixalite away with his claws, risking a bit of discomfort perhaps, but creating a large area from which he could hang upside down and feed.

So I decided to obtain yet another feeder—and this time I was going to place it entirely out of reach of the squirrel by attaching it to the end of a long pole which I secured to the molding on the side of the window. The pole, made of steel and aluminum, extended up at a 45° angle. My feeder was now about ten inches from the apartment building's wall; only if the squirrel could fly could he get to the feeder.

He can fly, I thought.

And perform other tricks as well. The squirrel now had a choice between leaping from the side of the building to the top of the feeder or shimmying up the pole to the feeder. Great, I thought, I've made things even easier for the little rodent. Well, if the squirrel can discover a simple solution, so can I: Nixalite on the top of the feeder would keep the squirrel off. And it did! Hurrah! I watched with glee as Mr. Squirrel climbed the pole, extended his paw to test the consistency of the feeder's roof, and determined that it was just too pointy—too risky—to sit on.

Needless to say I was very surprised and upset when I walked into my apartment the next afternoon and found a very—very—elongated squirrel connected like a bridge between the building's wall and the feeder. With back claws on the wall and front claws on the feeder, Mr. Squirrel's mouth was happily munching away.

By now I had disposed of my dart gun; now ideas came to mind like blasting him with Formula 409, or running an electrical current to feeder so that when the squirrel made his bridge, he would complete the circuit.

Instead, I rotated the feeder so that the long ends—the sides with the seed—were unreachable from the wall. To prevent the wind, or the squirrel, from rotating the feeder 90° for easy access, I secured it in place with a copper wire attached to the feeder and the brick wall. (Another of the many uses of copper bell wire—one of the few things squirrels can't chew through, though not from the lack of trying.) Although this meant that I couldn't see the birds that were eating on the far side of the feeder, away from the window, neither could the squirrel reach the food. Still, I could watch the birds fly around and perch on the pole. And the squirrel was absolutely frustrated by this—until he figured out that he could stretch just as easily from the window screen to the feeder, as he could from the wall to the feeder. It appeared to the squirrel—and to me—that the tiny grating that comprises the screen was designed to be a perfect match for the squirrel's claws. And I wasn't about to go without a screen; as much as I disliked squirrels, I hated mosquitoes even more.

So there we were: a standoff. Yes, I know—not exactly a standoff. Actually, the squirrel had won. The electric current idea seemed more attractive than ever, and I even went as far as visiting my local Radio Shack to explore the various paraphernalia—capacitors, more bell wire, waterproof batteries—that would make it work. It was tempting, but deep down I knew that, even though the squirrel wouldn't be electrocuted by such a system, only scared, it wasn't right. (Besides, despite my best efforts, I might accidentally zap a cardinal.)

I was angry! Frustrated! Not since college, when one of my hallmates stole my towel and room keys while I was in the shower, had I been outwitted by a creature with a brain the size of a walnut.

I ransacked my apartment for devices that could be used to battle the squirrel. I tried the strobe flash from my camera. I figured if people don't like being momentarily blinded with a flash, squirrels probably don't either. Well, you know all those photographs of cute squirrels you see in newspapers, magazines, and slide shows you're forced to watch? All those pictures are there because squirrels enjoy having their photos taken. Shoot a squirrel with a flash, and he puts on a squirrel-smile and stares at the camera, ready for another.

Once again, the only solution I could think of was what I've come to term "The Department of Defense Solution"—buying a much more expensive feeder. This time I chose the GSP feeder, manufactured by the Clarke Products Company. The GSP is the king of feeders, very sleek, even "high-tech" looking. The feeder is a lucite dome; birdseed fills a clear, hollow cavity within the walls of the dome. On top of the dome is an aluminum cover, which slides up to reveal an opening through which the birdseed is replenished. Because the feeder hangs in the air and because the only way in is through the space at the GSP's bottom, the only creatures which can enter the feeder are those with wings. So I shelled out my sixty dollars and then set up the GSP feeder.

And my theory about squirrels not being able to fly was proved correct. The squirrel was very frustrated by this change of events; all his life it had succeeded in foiling humans, and now, at last, a human had won.

But not for long. Somehow, the squirrel figured out a way to lift the aluminum top—while standing on a smooth, downward sloping surface—and stick his head inside the opening that was intended for replenishing the feeder. And feast!

Well, here I was in possession of a sixty dollar so-called squirrel-proof feeder whose only purpose, best I could tell, was to serve as a coordination test for squirrels. I wrote to the Clarke Products company and received a pleasant letter informing me that my squirrel was one of three that had learned how to remove the top cover to the feeder. The others were in Connecticut and Illinois. Fortunately there was a solution, the letter said. Clarke Products sent me a latch that goes above the top, requiring any-one (or any creature) that wants to lift the top to use two hands. And we all know that squirrels can't do that.

But what they can do is stretch from the screen on my window, pull the feeder toward them, and hoist themselves into the feeder. They're pretty adept at that.

I countered by putting the feeder on an even longer pole, extending horizontally from the wall of my building. Now there was no way—repeat no way—the squirrels could enter the feeder.

And this time I was right. They tried for days. For weeks. They even tried into the evening hours, when the fragile light was flittering away quickly into dangerous darkness, when squirrels want only to be safe in their nests. But they never could do it; my feeder was perfectly safe from Mr. Squirrel and his friends.

A few weeks later I read in one of those bird books that it's a good idea to have two feeders with different food in each because you attract more birds that way. So I attached another feeder to my window . . .

(This feeder and others are reviewed in Chapter 5, Rating the Feeders.)

Drawing by Stevenson; © *1988 The New Yorker Magazine, Inc.*

2

Attracting Birds and Bird Personalities

Compared to outwitting squirrels, attracting birds to your feeder is virtually effortless. All you have to do is put out some seed, peanut butter, nuts, bread crumbs, or fruit—and birds will flock your way like people to a "50 percent off" sale. Leave the food on your porch, put it in a bowl or tack the food to a tree—that's all you need to do if you want birds in your back yard. This is called the minimalist approach. You don't even need a feeder. However, buying a feeder helps keep the birdfeeder companies in business, and without them there would be no wonderful color catalogs of birds and birding supplies. For this if for no other reason, feeders are essential.

Besides encouraging the proliferation of catalogs, there are several advantages to using a feeder instead of throwing seed on the ground. Seed on the ground gets eaten by anything that crawls; feeders provide a modicum of squirrel protection; many birds don't like to feed on the ground, preferring instead to eat above ground; feeders protect seed from rain, snow and wind; feeders keep seed from getting all over the place.

Feeders and Food Beyond the minimalist, throw-seed-and-watch approach, there are many ways you can increase the number of birds that visit your yard and ways you can coax your favorite species to your feeder. The first step, of course, is a feeder; the second step is the right feeder. Chapter 5, Rating the Feeders, contains the most comprehensive discussion of feeders available anywhere and tells you which feeders are best for attracting which birds. Some important points to keep in mind regarding feeders are:

Keep your feeder full all year long. If you periodically let your feeder run out of feed, birds are going to seek their meals elsewhere. Birds—especially "desirable" ones such as cardinals and woodpeckers—develop loyalties to a particular area. They like to get to know an area they feel "safe" in. Birds build their nests where they become accustomed to the surroundings, where they know how to find emergency shelter if a cat or man wearing bright orange approaches. Some birds, such as red-bellied woodpeckers, appear so infrequently that if you want to attract them you'll have to provide chow all the time. Despite what you may have heard from your non-birding friends, it's okay to feed birds throughout the year. If you've heard that you shouldn't feed birds in the summer because they'll become dependent on you, regard such utterances as nonsense. You'll bring no harm to birds by offering them seed year round. The truth is that birds do much better because people feed them. In a sense they do depend on feeders. Not on you necessarily, but on people who feed birds in general; if your feeder closes down, there's bound to be someone else down the road who's more generous, and "your" birds will go there.

If you feed birds year round you will encourage them to nest near you. That's another good incentive.

But the most important reason to feed birds all year long is that as we turn more and more woodlands into shopping malls and highways, birds' natural sources of food disappear. Bird feeders like yourself are taking on nature's responsibility: you are helping birds survive and prosper. So feed all year long and enjoy.

As the seasons change, your feeding habits should change, too. Suet, hardened fat, is a terrific winter food that's enjoyed by just about every bird and adored by woodpeckers, but it doesn't hold up too well in summer. Suet, especially the home-brewed kind, can turn rancid in warm weather, so if you use it in summer, check it periodically. You may have to replace it before the suet gets eaten. (Alternatively, you can use suet as a squirrel diverter; it will be quickly consumed that way. See Chapter 6 for more information about diverting squirrels.) Sometime in April or May, depending on where you live, hummingbirds appear. They follow the flowers north. As soon as red flowers come up you should put out a hummingbird feeder—these are wonderful birds to watch.

Clean your feeder frequently. Mold and fungi can grow in a feeder, especially after a rain, and turn yummy birdseed into deadly birdseed. Cleaning your feeder has another advantage: it gets the dirt and bird dropping off and lets you see the birds more easily.

There are three categories of feeders: window, hanging, and pole feeders. Window feeders attach to windows with suction cups. They can be filled with a variety of seeds and offer the closest view of birds. Birding stores and mail order houses sell one-way transparent film you can place over your window so that you can see the birds, but they can't see you. Window feeders are squirrel-resistant only if one of two conditions are met: A) there are no squirrels around or B) the feeder is surrounded by a sufficiently large area of glass. Squirrels can't climb glass. Hanging feeders come in dozens of different shapes, and in a range of squirrel-proofness. They can be suspended from trees, specially-designed poles, brackets that extend from houses or fences, or from a wire strung between two trees. Never hang a feeder from an electrical or telephone wire; squirrels sometimes chew through the wires that support feeders. (Unless you like the taste of grilled squirrel.) Pole-mounted feeders are designed to be placed on a pole or post. When properly baffled they can be very squirrel-proof. These three feeder types enable you to place feeders just about anywhere you want. Chapter 5 discusses the placement of feeders in more detail.

George Petrides of the Wild Bird Center in Cabin John, Maryland said that if you want to triple the number of birds you attract, "double the number of feeders." He also pointed out that if you put different food in each of the feeders, you'll do even better.

What to fill your feeder with? There are over a dozen foods that birds like and that you can easily purchase. Oil sunflower seeds, fruit, peanuts, and suet are among their favorites. What you put in your feeders will affect the species of birds you attract.

And birds tastes vary from season to season. A wren, for example, may eat hulled sunflower seed in the winter, but shun it in the summer.

I've divided birdseed into three categories, Universal Food, Specialty Food, and Gourmet Food.

Inside the Wild Bird Center in Potomac, Maryland: there's a feeder for every fancy.

Universal Food Universal birdseed attracts just about every variety of bird, and every bird will eat it if hungry enough. Universal seed includes perodovic sunflower seed, sunflower hearts, and peanut hearts. Mix them together and it'll look like a scene from Alfred Hitchcock's *The Birds* around your feeder.

Specialty Seed Specialty seed attracts only a handful of specific birds, and, perhaps more significantly, is disliked by certain birds. Safflower seed, for example, gets gobbled down by chickadees and finches, but starlings and grackles hate it; chickadees, nuthatches and titmice love shelled peanuts, while finches aren't too crazy about them. Most ground-feeding birds like millet, while birds that feed from hanging feeders will usually toss the millet aside. Other specialty seeds include yellow corn and canary seed.

Gourmet Seed Gourmet seed attracts only a very small number of birds and is expensive. Thistle seed, which brings in finches and can be used to attract goldfinches in particular, falls into this category. Raspberries and orange slices are other gourmet foods.

SEEDS AND THE BIRDS THEY ATTRACT

Sunflower Seed
Titmice
Nuthatches
Cardinals
Finches
Chickadees
Grosbeaks
Crossbills
Starlings
Sparrows
Mourning doves

Sunflower Hearts
Chickadees
Cardinals
Nuthatches
Goldfinches
House finches
Redpolls
Blackbirds
Juncos
Wrens
Sparrows
Mourning doves

Fruit
Mockingbirds
Orioles

Suet
Downy
woodpeckers
Red-headed
woodpeckers
Red-bellied
woodpeckers
Chickadees
Titmice
Nuthatches

Safflower Seed
(Starlings and grackles don't like safflower seeds)
Cardinals
Purple finches
Titmice
Chickadees

Thistle Seed
Goldfinches
Purple finches
House finches
Redpolls
Juncos
Indigo Buntings
Pine Siskins

Shelled Peanuts
Blue Jays
Woodpeckers
Grosbeaks
Titmice
Chickadees
Cardinals
Towhees
Nuthatches

Whole Peanuts
Blue Jays
Titmice

White Proso Millet
Pine Siskins
Mourning doves
Juncos
Purple finches

Avoid commercial seed mixes sold in supermarkets and hardware stores that contain large amounts of millet and other less desirable seed. When a bird encounters a seed it doesn't want, it flicks that seed aside; people who fill their feeders with mixed seed containing millet usually find the ground beneath their feeder covered with millet. A much better idea is to erect two or three feeders, each with one kind of seed.

Water Birds must have water to drink and bathe in. Water is so important to them that you can attract birds to your yard with a water station alone.

Plenty of commercial birdbaths are available, but you can just as easily construct your own. A clay plant dish makes an excellent birdbath, as does a window birdfeeder, or an aluminum trashcan lid turned upside down. Make sure your water station isn't too deep—3 inches is the maximum. If the water is too deep, birds may have trouble escaping in an emergency, such as a cat attack. Be sure to locate your water station away from any place these cats could hide. If you can put the birdbath on top of a baffled pole, that's even better. Give the bath a gradual slope by putting stones and pebbles along the outer rim.

Birds need water all year long, so don't neglect the birdbath in winter. Some catalogs and stores such as Duncraft and The Audubon Workshop sell heated birdbaths.

You're going to have to clean your birdbath from time to time unless it rains enough to wash the bath out. Bacteria and algae can grow rapidly in a birdbath.

Finally, squirrels like to drink from birdbaths, too. You can try to prevent squirrels from getting to your water station if you want, but water's inexpensive enough that this probably isn't worth the effort.

Nests and Boxes You've probably noticed that birds like to rise early, sometimes causing you to awaken before your cells are ready. But when they're not active, birds do the same thing that you do. They sleep. This they do in nests, and the more nesting areas you have around your house, the more birds there will be.

You've already enticed birds to your yard by feeding them, so they're predisposed to set up home. You can encourage them to homestead either by providing them with nesting material, or by putting up birdhouses. Duncraft and The Wild Bird Center (listed in the back of the book) sell nesting material you can hang from a tree. Commercial nesting material consists of twine, cotton, sisal, hemp, and yarn—for birds these materials are a good adjunct to what they find from nature. You can also leave out thread and twigs for birds to build nests from. Most birds, including chickadees, goldfinches, robins, and orioles, use this material.

Commercial birdhouses are available in a variety of shapes. Different species prefer different kind of houses; they have different tastes when it comes to entrance size, space inside, and "look." Chickadees, downy woodpeckers, nuthatches, wrens, barn owls, bluebirds and purple martins love to live in man-made houses. The Audubon Workshop, Duncraft, and Wild Bird Center all offer a wide variety of birdhouses. If you're looking for a birdhouse that will impress the neighbors, Richard Clark, owner of The Bird House, hand makes birdhouses that look more like art.

You can also build birdhouses. Milk cartons with 1″ holes near the top make excellent temporary nesting sites. If you're going to construct a birdhouse, make sure the wood is 3/4 to 1 inch thick and that it is treated with a wood preservative, or at the very least, paint.

Whichever birdhouse you buy, be sure to protect it from predators. Squirrels eat baby birds and eggs. Cats like to patrol around birdhouses—so make certain that all they can do is watch. Putting the birdhouse on top of a baffled pole is a good idea; Nixalite can also help keep cats and other predators away. Birdhouses must be securely mounted; when they fall baby birds die. If the tenants leave for summer or winter vacation, take that opportunity to clean the birdhouse. Make sure that rain can't spill inside, or that there are drainage holes in your birdhouse. Ventilation should be adequate, and the birdhouse shouldn't be placed in a place where it receives direct sun during the hottest part of the summer day.

The chart below shows the size of birdhouses that various birds prefer. Use this guide when building or buying a birdhouse. For all these birds, the entrance should be about 6 to 8 inches above the birdhouse's floor.

Birdhouse Preferences
(in inches)

	Floor Space	Depth	Entrance Hole Diameter
Bluebird	5 × 5	8	1½
Chickadee	4 × 4	8–10	1⅛
Downy Woodpecker	4 × 4	8–10	1¼
Crested Flycatcher	6 × 6	8–10	2
Nuthatch	4 × 4	8–10	1¼
Wren	4 × 4	6–8	1–1¼

Your Garden Have you ever wondered why New York City has few birds and why those that are there are congregated in Central Park? There's a clear relationship between the number of plants and flowers in your yard and the number of birds there. The ideal backyard for attracting birds is surrounded by trees and filled with shrubs and flowering plants. Dead trees help, too; if you have dead trees around **don't cut them down**. (If you do, make sure that there aren't any nests in the cavities. Replace dead trees with new ones. Of course, if a dead tree is threatening your house, the house takes priority.) Dead trees are excellent sources of food and shelter for many species of birds.

PERSONALITY PROFILES OF SOME COMMON BIRDS

Now that you know how easy it is to attract birds of different species to your yard, it's worth knowing a little about how these birds behave and what they expect of you. As you spend more and more time at your feeder—and you will, it's an addicting hobby—you'll notice that each species not only looks different, but has its own personality, preferred feeding time, and way of eating. The sketches below are only intended to introduce you to these birds as birders know them. For more detailed information, consult the books listed in Resources.

Chickadee Of the various kinds of chickadees, the black-capped is the most familiar. It is one of the smallest and friendliest birds to visit feeders—a chickadee will eat out of your hand if you're patient. Chickadees weigh about 1/3 of an ounce, the same as four pennies. They are predominantly black with a black cap, white cheeks, and a white-yellow underbelly.

Chickadees are fun to watch. They zip over to your feeder, grab a nut or sunflower seed, then fly to a tree to eat; as soon as they're finished they fly right back. They are constantly active, hopping from tree to feeder to branch; if they were people, they'd probably be offered a sedative. Chickadees will eat whole nuts, sunflower and safflower seeds, suet—pretty much anything. They will eat from platform feeders, hanging feeders and pole-mounted feeders. Because of their size you can frequently adjust feeders to allow chickadees in, but prevent larger birds from getting the seed.

In flight, chickadees are acrobats. They can change directions in mid-air in 3/100 of a second. You'll never get bored watching them. Naturalist George Harrison, in *The Backyard Birdwatcher,* writes, "If there is such a thing as reincarnation, I want to come back as a chickadee" (Simon and Schuster, 1979).

Tufted Titmouse
Both the titmouse and chickadee are part of the titmouse family, and their behavior is similar. Like the chickadee, the tufted titmouse has a fun-loving, spirited personality. With its diminutive size, strong-looking face and beak, gray back, white belly and tufted top (its crest), the titmouse is probably the cutest bird that visits feeders. They walk and explore the area around your feeder, turning their heads from side to side, raising and lowering their crest. They do this with a quizzical look, as if they are trying to communicate with you.

Titmice are loyal birds, and will stay near a feeder all year long. They are particularly common during winter. Although not as tameable as chickadees, you may be able to get titmice to eat out of your hand.

Like the chickadee, the tufted titmouse usually grabs a seed, then takes it away and eats on a branch. They'll even do this with a whole peanut—it's an amusing sight to watch a bird carry a nut that's about 1/5 its size. Titmice pound the seed against the branch to get it open. A friend of mine, Yvonne Lodico, watching this action and noting the titmice's unusual crest, dubbed these birds, "hammerhead birds."

Cardinal The cardinal is the bird that many high school, college and some professional sports teams make its mascot, which is something that surprises most birders. Although the cardinal is among the most beautiful birds attracted to feeders, it is timid and aloof. However, cardinals are territorial, and during mating season will bully their rivals to drive them off. I guess this may give them something in common with the individual players on sports teams.

Male cardinals are brilliantly red with a crest. Female cardinals have the same crest, but are rose-colored. In winter cardinals travel in flocks, so if you have one you're likely to have several at your feeder; but during the midspring to summer breeding season you'll see cardinals either alone or in pairs. Cardinals don't migrate.

Cardinals are ground-feeders, so you're not likely to find them on a perch at a hanging feeder. Platform feeders filled with sun-flower seed (their favorite food) or seed that spills from other feeders will attract cardinals. Nuts, safflower seed, and cracked corn may also appeal to cardinals. These birds prefer to snack early in the morning or just before dark; however during bad weather and winter they will appear at feeders throughout the day. If cardinals survive childhood, they may live three years in the wild.

Downy Woodpecker The downy woodpecker is the smallest and tamest American woodpecker, and is a frequent visitor to feeders. When not hammering small holes in your house early in the morn-ing and especially on weekend mornings, downy woodpeckers enjoy beef suet (but will also eat sunflower seeds and whole pea-nuts). A regular supply of beef suet may keep them from turning your house into a toothpick factory.

When you hear a downy—or other woodpecker—go tap tap tap it may be doing one of two things. Irregular tapping noise means the woodpecker is looking for food, and you've run out of suet. A regular drumming sound is a signal that usually occurs during breeding season, and probably won't damage your house.

The downy is about the size of a house sparrow, with a larger beak and longer tail. It has black and white markings; the male has a red patch on its head.

Downies are found throughout North America. They make their nests between 3 and 50 feet above the ground on the bottom side of tree limbs. Downy woodpeckers will help clear your garden of undesirable insects, so attract as many as you can. A healthy downy can live over ten years.

House Wren An adorable little brown bird, the house wren doesn't seem to mind being around people and houses. It nests comfortably in store-bought nesting boxes, in home-made boxes fabricated from milk cartons, or in old shoes and discarded couches.

The wren has an assertive, energetic personality. Despite its small size, the house wren has an aggressive nature when it comes to nests. The males will often fly from nesting box to nesting box in their territory, decorating the interior so that other birds think the box is full. A wren will also follow a downy woodpecker to its nest and may even chase away a pair of downies it finds there. When a wren decides that it wants to nest somewhere, nothing will drive it away.

Wrens eat mostly insects, but are drawn by suet, cornbread and hulled sunflower seed in the colder months. Once in your yard, they're likely to remain there (and help you keep your insect population down).

House Finch On alternating days my friend Stephanie Faul decides that "the finches are okay because it's nice to have any kind of bird at the feeder," or "I wish all those noisy finches would go away." But she adds, "My cat Travis thinks they are great. For any cat, finches are kitty T.V." If there's one thing about finches, its that there's no such thing as one finch. They arrive in groups so large that you have to remove your shoes and socks to count them. Finches will crowd closely together at a feeder as they eat— I once saw seven side by side at the SPF feeder in our yard.

House finches are lively, aggressive birds. They will scream and poke at each other for space at the feeder, and sometimes carry on this quarreling in midflight. I've seen house finches successfully challenge downy woodpeckers and chickadees for a position at the feeder.

Still, they are vivacious and a spectacular. They're constantly in motion, constantly sounding off; and while they are far from charming to the eye, the males sport a bright red breast that puts house finches in the category of "fairly attractive" birds. Females, alas, are nondescript.

House finches were originally native only to the western United States. But in the 1940s pet dealers in California captured some of these birds and had them sold in New York City as "Hollywood birds." It didn't take long for U.S. Fish and Wildlife officials to catch up with these cage-bird dealers—selling these wild birds was illegal. Some dealers released their house finches, where they survived and prospered.

House finches will nest almost anywhere. They will eat almost anything, although they aren't terribly fond of cracked corn, millet, and hulled oats. Unfortunately finches rarely eat insects, so they won't do anything to reduce the number of mosquito bites you receive each year.

One of the most interesting features of house finches is the way they move together. A flock will be eating at a feeder and then suddenly—seemingly without reason—fly away. And then just as suddenly they will return.

The best time to observe house finches is in late March and early April during mating season. To entice females, males do a bit of a song and dance and then feed the females. At feeders you can watch females crane their necks back, open their mouths and wait for males to put seed in it. It's a wonderful sight.

A flock of finches can empty a feeder faster than a squirrel can.

Mourning Dove ohCooo ohCooo ohCooo. The mourning dove is a cousin of the—dare I speak the word—pigeon, but fortunately there's little significant family resemblance. (A closer cousin is the extinct passenger pigeon.) Mourning doves make one of the most satisfying sounds—the dove's soft melody is like a natural Valium. In the winter mourning doves travel in flocks of about 20, but they nest as pairs.

Mourning doves are twelve inches long, sleeker than pigeons, and have pointed tails. They have a rust-beige head and breast, and gray tailfeathers specked with white and black.

Mourning doves are ground-feeding birds (their favorite food is cracked corn but they like millet and black sunflower, too) so that is where you will usually see them. They are exceptional fliers, and have been clocked at up to 60 mph. Although they are widely hunted as a game bird, mourning doves are a successful species, with an estimated 500 million throughout the United States. Their range extends north into Alaska and south to Panama.

Doves will defend their territory against other birds while nesting, but they are usually shy birds. They quickly launch into the air at the earliest sign of danger.

Starling People who like starlings are also squirrel lovers. I don't say that based on a formal study, but it seems to make sense. I'm sure you'll agree.

Starlings are a regular pain at feeders. Most likely a comment like that won't win me any points in the die-hard birding community, which treats all feathered creatures with the utmost adoration, but 99 percent of birdfeeder owners would rather not have them. Starlings are noisy, aggressive, and not terribly pleasing to look at. They chase away other birds, eat plenty of birdseed and make a big mess at feeders. (Then the squirrels arrive to mop the spilled seed from the ground.)

Starlings are not native to America, as you probably guessed by the way they respond to our hospitality. They were brought over from Europe in 1890 by birders who thought starlings would make a welcome addition—like perfume or something. Sixty pairs were released in Central Park. As soon as they could they left New York City and within fifty years had spread across the country.

Starlings are one of the few birds that dramatically change appearance over the year. In the winter their black feathers are covered with specks of white that look like Vs. In summer they are mostly black and iridescent green. Starlings roost in large numbers—dozens of birds. They're awkward fliers and shun wooded areas. They will invade nesting boxes with holes larger than 2″. Starlings love suet, peanut hearts, bakery goods and cracked corn. They shun thistle, whole peanuts and sunflower seeds.

One fascinating aspect of starling behavior, however, is the way they gather in flocks. Sometimes you can see hundreds of starlings circling a small area, flying round and round for an hour. It's a fascinating sight.

Starlings are smart. It's rumored that you can even teach a starling to talk like a parrot.

Pigeon Not a bird. Put here by mistake.

Goldfinch If you want to know how arbitrary humans can be, just measure their reaction to the goldfinch versus house finch. The major difference between goldfinches and house finches is color. The goldfinch's bright gold feathers (which become grayish-yellow in winter after molting) are a stark contrast to the house finch's drab looks. They are both around the same size, have many similar behavior traits, eat the same seed, and eat in the same manner—they gorge themselves.

Entire chapters in bird books are devoted to goldfinches, but house and purple finches usually get grouped under the heading "other birds." I'm not trying to defend house finches—I'm wooed by goldies' looks like every other feeder—and I certainly think that house finches eat far more seed than they deserve. I just want to be honest.

Goldfinches are sometimes mistakenly called "wild canaries" because of their color and their song. If you want to draw goldfinches put out niger (thistle) seed; although goldfinches like black sunflower seed, they will travel anywhere for thistle. So much do they love it, you could probably attract them into your house with a trail of thistle. Goldfinches prefer to eat at perches. If you want to deter house finches, cut the perches on your hanging feeder to about 1/3"; the goldfinches can grab on, but house finches can't maintain their balance and eat. Goldfinches like to live in open areas such as orchards beside roads and in swamps. Man's clearing of woodlands has encouraged their spread. In the wild they thrive on thistle and insects. In September the goldfinch's feathers molt, changing from gold to a dark olive color.

Goldfinches are not territorial. Instead they are tolerant of other species of birds, even during breeding season.

The goldfinch is the state bird of Iowa, New Jersey and Washington.

Nuthatch Small children and adults from New York call the nuthatch "the upside-down bird," because it can often be seen climbing down trees upside down. It's unusually designed feet enable it to walk down, head first. Most birds have four toes, three in the front and one in the back. The nuthatch has two on either side. This ability enables nuthatches to capture many insects that other birds miss on trees.

The nuthatch is bluish-gray—not spectacular like the cardinal or blue jay, but a pretty bird. Its call, **ank ank ank**, is distinctive. The white-breasted nuthatch is the largest and most common nuthatch in North America. The red-breasted nuthatch is usually found in the forests of the West and north of the Great Lakes.

Nuthatches live in cavities or abandoned woodpecker holes of trees. They eat plenty of insects in summer, and in the winter are frequent visitors to feeding stations, where they consume sunflower seeds, sunflower hearts, suet, and shelled peanuts.

Nuthatches' range extends up to 50 acres. Like chickadees and titmice, nuthatches aren't bothered by human company—they can be tamed to eat sunflower seed out of your hand. Some people even claim that nuthatches can be trained to get used to particular individuals so that they come when called by that person.

Blue Jay I have to admit a bias. I'm partial to the blue jay. Like its western cousin, the striking Steller's jay, the blue is one of the most beautiful birds that visits feeders. Within the birding community there's a debate over which is more beautiful, the cardinal or blue jay. The verdict is not in.

Blue jays are about 12 inches long, and are covered mostly with blue feathers. Around their neck is a "bright" band of black. The blue jay's iridescent color isn't entirely intrinsic to the bird's feathers; in certain lights blue jays appear almost colorless.

Blue jays receive a lot of bad press. They're blamed for scaring other birds away from feeders with their aggressive approach. Jays can imitate the sound of hawks. There's another myth that a blue jay will give a fake warning call when it arrives at a feeder to give the impression that danger abounds. Both assertions have only marginal truth. Jays sometimes frighten other birds, but are no more aggressive than house finches, and given their relative size, blue jays can even be considered docile. Jays don't hang around feeders for long periods of time, either. If blue jays are disrupting your feeder, put a separate feeder aside for jays and fill it with peanuts. As for the "false alarm" myth—sometimes jays will squawk as they approach a feeding station, but other birds either learn to ignore this or simply wait a couple of minutes before returning to the feeder.

The striking blue jay.

There are those who claim that blue jays raid nests, eat eggs, and occasionally eat young birds. These claims come from the same people who have explored the interiors of UFOs.

Blue jays are protective parents. They will attack any creature that approaches their nest. Some jays migrate south during the winter, others prefer to stay put.

To entice blue jays, it helps to have acorns in abundance. (Blue jays compete with squirrels for the acorn crop. The more jays the merrier.) Shelled or whole peanuts are their second favorite dish, followed by black sunflower seed and suet. Jays nest in shrubs and small, wide trees—the more plant cover, the better. Jays are fond of birdbaths, too.

Jays store food by burying nuts. You can also see them carrying several shelled nuts in their mouths at a time. The number of jays in any given year depends in large measure on the number of acorns during the previous season.

Junco The junco is one of people's favorites. It's handsome (not spectacular), doesn't make much noise, doesn't bother other birds, doesn't eat too much, doesn't spill seed around, and doesn't come in large flocks. In spring and summer juncos gorge themselves on insects and enjoy eating seeds that other birds shun such as red proso millet (their favorite), cracked corn, and canary seed. They also eat black sunflower seed and suet. Juncos are primarily ground-feeding birds.

The junco also goes by the name "snowbird" because it usually appears at feeders at the first snow. It lives in the northern, western and eastern parts of the United States, journeying south during winter. The junco is not only well-behaved, but has a sense of loyalty, too, and will return to the same feeder year after year. The junco likes to get up early.

In 1984, Lafayette Park, across the street from the White House, had more squirrels than any other place in the world. "The density of squirrels in that park is the highest ever recorded in the scientific literature," said David Manski, an urban wildlife biologist. There were an estimated 120 squirrels in the eight-acre park, thanks in large part to tourists and residents who feed them every day. One Washington resident confessed to spending between $60 and $90 a week on nuts for squirrels. These "volunteer feeders" provide 75 percent of park squirrels' diets in winter. U.S. Park officials resorted to squirrel-napping and moved squirrels to other Washington parks to reduce the number of squirrels in Lafayette Park.

3

Know The Enemy: Everything a Birdfeeder Needs to Know About Squirrels

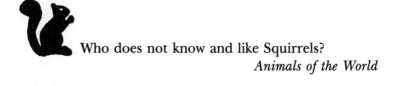 Who does not know and like Squirrels?
Animals of the World

The large gray squirrel (*Sciurus Carolinesis*) I do not find as plentiful in Campton [Massachusetts] as the other two species; for several seasons past, very few have appeared in the wood or on the roadside. In Roxbury, a part of Boston, they are quite common among the trees on some of the old estates, and they are often seen in the hemlock grove in the Arnold aboretum. Nothing can be more graceful than their scalloped lines of flight along a tree bough.

The gray squirrel is a sociable little animal who likes the company of a man with a few nuts in his pocket. One cannot walk across the square in Richmond, Va., without encountering two or three tame individuals who regard a man as a species of animated nut tree created for his especial benefit!

If we will watch a squirrel closely we may observe him tuck away two or three small nuts in his cheeks and carry another in his teeth. Last summer one of my friendly chipmunks made six journeys within two hours from a certain corner of the house to his nest beneath a fence post by the road, for the purpose of transferring his summer stores. One would suppose upon beholding his bulgy cheeks that he was afflicted with a severe form of mumps.
—F. Schuyler Mathews, *Familiar Features of the Roadside*

If you're going to do battle with squirrels, you're going to lose every time—unless you know as much about them as you possibly can. Intelligence is frequently 90 percent of any war—and the war against squirrels is no exception. The Japanese knew all about Pearl Harbor in 1941. Israel's victory in 1967 was due in large measure to superior Israeli intelligence. The Soviet bugging of the U.S. Embassy in Moscow rendered our embassy virtually useless for confidential work. Mata Hari was famous only because she gathered facts. Regular soldiers may be interned in prisoner of war camps during wartime, but spies are shot because one scrap of useful information about the enemy can be worth a thousand soldiers.

I repeat: you have to know everything about squirrels. Because they know everything about you.

Squirrels know that when you fill a feeder, you're ringing the dinner bell for them. Squirrels know that you're going to put baffles on top of feeders, so in the meanwhile they practice their jumping skills. Squirrels know that you may occasionally scream and flail your arms at them, but that in a few minutes you'll go away. Squirrels know that if they gnaw through one feeder, you'll buy another for them to sharpen their teeth on. Squirrels know that if you string a feeder between two trees on a thin wire, they've rehearsed their tightrope-walking skills. Squirrels know that if they eat the feed you've put out for birds, you'll just put out

Gray Squirrel Fact Sheet

(Remember, you can't tell the players without a scorecard)

Latin name: Sciurus Carolinesis

Adult female weight: 16 to 24 ounces

Adult male weight: 16 to 24 ounces

Length: 8 to 11 inches long with a tail that measures 8 to 10 inches

Home range size: 1 to 7 acres (some biologists report that squirrel ranges extend to 20 acres).

Number of plant species eaten: 30–60 (most are eaten rarely; however, gardeners beware)

Foods: Tree nuts, plant seeds, fruit, flowers, mushrooms, buds, birdseed, peanut butter (preferably Skippy Super Chunk).

Percentage of food from animal matter (including bird eggs):   2–11 percent

Mean annual survival rate in the wild: 52 percent

Reproduction: Usually two litters a year.

Lifespan: About 1 year in the wild; up to 12 years as pets (which is far longer than the furniture survives).

more. Squirrels know not to attack your spouse, children and pets, because that might cause you to react violently. Squirrels know that no matter what, there's going to be delicious seed in your yard. Yes, indeed, squirrels know humans pretty well.

The gray squirrel is called *Sciurus carolinesis* by those who study them for a living. There are dozens of species of squirrels, some of them very cute. (There are 36 species of flying squirrels in Europe, Asia, North and Central America.) The cute squirrels stay in forests and eat only acorns, wild berries, hickory nuts and other foods that squirrels were originally supposed to eat. Squirrels are generally classified into two groups: those that dwell in trees, such as the gray squirrel, the flying squirrel (*Glaucomys volans*), the tassel-eared squirrel (*Sciurus aberti*), and the eastern fox squirrel (*Sciurus niger*) are called **tree squirrels**. The second group are **ground squirrels**—squirrels that think it isn't wise for a 10-inch-long animal to climb a 60-foot-tall tree, and consequently never venture up. These include the beautiful golden mantle squirrel.

Squirrels are members of the rodent family, sometimes called by zoologists the "order of gnawing animals." Rodent comes from the latin **rodere**, meaning to gnaw—and there are over 1,600 species of rodents. But there's a forest-wide difference between the various members of rodent family, which includes squirrels, beavers, rabbits, mice and rats. They behave differently, eat different foods and look different. (Which is a real blessing. Could you imagine how much more awful the squirrel problem would be if squirrels not only pilfered birdseed, but also looked like their distant relatives, rats?)

Squirrels evolved between 54 to 37 million years ago in North America during the Eocene epoch. Using the land bridges that existed between continents, squirrels may have spread to Africa during the Miocene era, some 25 to 5 million years ago, and into South America after the Panama land bridge formed about three million years ago, during the Pliocene era. Near the end of the Oligocene era, roughly 30 to 25 million years ago, squirrels diversified into true tree-and ground-dwelling squirrels, a metamorphosis that apparently came about because of changes in climate and vegetation. The origins of *Sciurus carolinesis*, the gray squirrel, are unknown.

Squirrels have only one thing to do all day long: eat. Practically every activity they're involved in concerns food. Their physical make-up enables them to be perpetual eating machines. A mere two percent of a squirrel's energy goes to making babies. (No Dr. Ruths in the squirrel world.) Just about all of the remaining 98 percent focuses on food. Your food. Squirrels are land sharks, living eating machines.

Squirrels and Food Squirrels eat a lot. You don't need a zoologist to tell you that. Adult gray squirrels consume roughly one and a half pounds of nuts or seed a week. That may not sound like a lot, but squirrels eat as much as or more than their entire body weight a week. (You try that and see what happens.) A mere four squirrels will polish off six pounds of birdseed a week. Squirrels can demolish about three ounces of food in one sitting, which means that four of them will empty a small one-pound feeder in the time it takes you to mail order more birdseed.

Crammed into the tiny squirrel is a 7-foot-long digestive tract, capable of handling a variety of foods. Squirrels'favorite fares, more or less in order of preference, are hickory nuts, pecans, black walnuts, and acorns. They enjoy just about every kind of nut and berry forests provide, including pine seed, corn, black gum fruits, sugar maple seeds, dogwood fruits, wild cherries, and beechnuts. Although acorns provide more nutrients for squirrels than do hickory nuts, they prefer the latter hands down. One of the reasons may be that the hickory nut's hard shell helps squirrels sharpen their teeth. Another may be because hickory nuts taste terrific. But more likely the reason is that hickory nuts have a very high fat content, 29 percent, and fat is essential to a squirrel's nutrition. According to naturalist and writer Ernest Thompson Seton, a squirrel's love for hickory nuts

> . . . amounts almost to a passion. He will pass by all other foods, and brave innumerable dangers for a feast of his favorites. So eager is he for the annual bounty of his mother tree, that he cannot await the decent time of ripening, but cuts them while they are green. He is like an overeager, overgreedy small boy who is too impatient to wait for the thorough baking of his cake, so nibbles and nibbles at the unsatisfactory, unwholesome dough (*Life*

Histories of Northern Animals, Charles Scribner's Sons, 1909).

In all, there are over seven major squirrel foods. Gray squirrels will eat between 30 and 60 different plants. (Compare that to the average American, whose major sustenance consists of a Big Mac, fries, and Coke, with occasional experimentations with exotic dishes such as chili dogs or onion dip.)

Acorns, however, are among the most important food for gray squirrels, both the city and forest varieties. Oak trees go through five-year cycles of acorn production, and as a result squirrel populations go through five-year cycles. You can predict how many baby squirrels there are going to be by the acorn crop.

Which birdseed do squirrels like best? An experiment was conducted at the Schlitz Audubon Center in Milwaukee, Wisconsin to test birds' preferences for seed. Twelve Droll Yankee feeders were strung along a wire, each filled with a different seed. The entire apparatus was protected by various baffles. The birds never had a chance. Within minutes several gray squirrels attacked the feeders. The researchers discovered that *squirrels* prefer black sunflower seeds; once sunflower seeds are gone, squirrels begin on other seed. Squirrels are not too fond of thistle; however, they will eat thistle when they're hungry enough. Gray squirrels prefer white acorns to red and black acorns, when given a choice, possibly because of the relatively high tannin content of red and black acorns. Tannin may make acorns less tasty and less digestible.

Gray squirrels are omnivorous. In addition to vegetable matter, such as berries and nuts, they eat minerals and animals. Squirrels also strip bark on trees, possibly for several reasons: to sharpen their teeth, to obtain some of the nutrients in the sappy tissue beneath the bark, to gather material to line their nests with, and as a behavioral characteristic.

Gray squirrels have earned the term **tree rat** because of the damage they do to hardwood trees by stripping bark. They gnaw at the bark until they make a hole, then use this notch to strip the bark off by pulling on it. Occasionally squirrels will kill a tree by stripping the bark around a tree's entire circumference. Other times, bark stripping makes trees susceptible to a variety of fungal diseases. The problem of bark stripping is particularly prevalent in England, where the European sycamore and European beech have been severely damaged in tree plantations. Squirrels also eat buds and shoots on trees, damaging new growth.

Squirrels also eat mushrooms, including the deadly amanita, apparently for the nutrients they offer. They have no problem with nontraditional foods either. Apples, peanut butter, peanut M&Ms (they don't seem to like red ones), and corn on the cob, buttered or unbuttered, meet their requirements for taste.

Squirrels will also eat bird eggs, baby birds and the bones of dead mammals. Approximately 10 percent of their diet comes from animal matter, which also includes insects. Apparently squirrels derive some nutrients, probably calcium, from these meats.

Although squirrels obtain some of the water they need from non-nut foods such as berries, fruits and grasses, squirrels must drink water twice a day. You'll notice that squirrels visit your birdbath as often as birds do. In winter squirrels will eat snow for water.

A squirrel's teeth are its most important tool. Two pairs of surgically sharp incisors enable squirrels to gnaw through the outside of any nut, and practically any substance. Wood and plastic pose no problem for squirrels; squirrels can even make holes in certain kinds of metal. My friend, Peggy Robin, swears that a squirrel gnawed through the telephone wire that her feeder was hanging from. Flesh, as I unfortunately discovered while examining a squirrel closely, is the easiest material for squirrels to bite through. A squirrel's incisors grow about six inches a year, and must constantly be worn down by eating or chewing on various objects like fence posts and fingers. If a squirrel looses its teeth, or if it suffers a malocclusion, that's the equivalent of a death sentence.

After the squirrel uses its incisors to cut and strip the food, it passes to four pairs of premolars, which look like pegs, where it is ground into fine fragments. Peeling is an important part of the eating process. If you watch a squirrel eat a raw peanut or acorn, you'll see how it carefully strips away the undesirable parts. Squirrel jaws make two motions. First, the lower jaw is pulled forward so that the bottom and top incisors can gnaw the food, then the lower jaw pulls back so the cheek teeth can grind the food.

Gray squirrels prefer to dine while sitting on their back legs, but can eat from any position, including upside down. A squirrel hanging from its back legs, its paws wrapped around a chain with a sunflower seed in its front paws, is a common sight among birders. Squirrels can even eat when their bodies are stretched very long between a tree and a feeder. Squirrels bury nuts to store food for winter, when there's little natural food. That's not news. What is interesting is that despite squirrels' intense interest in food, squirrels cannot remember where they've buried a nut for more than twenty minutes. Not very smart animals, after all, it seems. Or are they? Although squirrels don't know where their nuts are buried, they have no problem locating nuts that they or other squirrels have buried. Squirrels locate buried nuts using their sense of smell, and can find nuts buried under several inches of snow. In fact, most of the nuts a squirrel recovers will not be the ones it buried. Caching nuts is one of their most important survival instincts. Squirrels bury nuts communally so that all members of the species in the area benefit. Almost as soon as they leave the nest, young squirrels start burying nuts, although at first they don't completely cover the nut.

Squirrels can bury up to twenty-five nuts an hour. They bury nuts over a widely scattered area; this is called scatterhoarding.

There's another advantage to scatterhoarding besides providing nuts for other squirrels. There are many other species that forage for buried nuts, but if a competing species finds many nuts in a small area it will probably stay there. However, scatterhoarding, with its low density of nuts, prevents competitors from finding a large cache, because there is none.

In semi-urban areas squirrels become desperate for places to bury nuts. According to the *Washington Post*, "an alarming number . . . have chosen to stockpile their nuts in electrical transformers at the top of power poles." The result: "Squirrels are getting zapped and electrical blackouts are increasing." In one day in the Washington area there were seven squirrel-inspired blackouts.

Squirrels' burying instinct is powerful. In the building where I have my writing studio there's a woman who feeds squirrels on her windowsill. She mentioned that squirrels occasionally come into her apartment through the window. They steal peanuts from her kitchen counter and bury them in her avocado plant.

Spring is a crucial season for squirrels, because during the winter they will have lost a considerable amount of weight. At the end of March, when squirrels weigh their lowest, they must seek new plant growth—buds, berries and stalks—and new bird-feeders. A squirrel's weight varies by as much as 25 percent between autumn and spring. That's some diet!

Physical Capabilities When you read a list describing the prowess of squirrels you think that they might be the supermen of the lower animals. They have immensely powerful hind legs. Squirrels can jump up six feet. They can leap between trees that are eight feet apart. They can climb up dozens of feet and scale just about every surface except glass. Glass is to squirrels as lead is to Superman. They're swift, too. Squirrels have been clocked at 19 miles per hour, definitely not faster than a speeding locomotive, but a heck of a lot swifter than many people. Squirrels can swim. Yes, swim. Up to a mile. To swim squirrels manage a variation of the dog paddle, keeping their heads above water and their tails either just above or on the surface of the water. Squirrels can dig up earth and burrow through snow to create tunnels.

Squirrels have acute senses. Their sense of smell is uncanny. Their hearing enables them to be aware of any changes in the flow of sounds in the woods. They can hear doors opening, a predator walking, or a feeder being filled. A squirrel's vision is also remarkably powerful, and its eyes, which are situated on opposite sides of its head, give the squirrel a wide range of vision without moving its head. It was once thought that gray squirrels had only cone cells in their eyes, but now researchers are sure they have rod cells (sensitive to light) near the center of their retina, and cone cells (for distinguishing colors) around the rods. This gives squirrels the ability to see fine detail including vertical objects, a necessity if you're leaping from tree to tree. It's said that one squirrel can distinguish another from a distance of 50 feet. Squirrel eyes also respond quickly to changes in their field of vision; they can see objects moving twice as fast as a human can. Grays possess dichromatic color vision (humans have trichromatic vision). They can't distinguish between red and green, which may help explain why so many never make it across the street.

Squirrels have two peak activity times during the day in the spring, summer, and fall: the first two hours after sunrise, and midafternoon. In the winter they are active only around noontime. In February they spend 73 percent of their time foraging for food; in August only 31 percent. Dawn is a more important signal for the start of squirrel activity than dusk is for ending it. In cold weather squirrels spend more time in their nests, and have been known to spend several days there during particularly severe weather. Squirrels become lethargic in hot weather, and may take a siesta in the middle of the day. Rain doesn't bother squirrels.

Squirrels mark travel lanes which they journey along, just as we might use a path. These lanes, which are on the ground and among branches in trees, are marked by scent from squirrels' glands. Because they know these paths, squirrels can swiftly leap from branch to branch, certain what lies ahead.

Squirrels molt—change their coats—twice a year, in spring and autumn. Molting starts at the nose and eyes and them moves in a fixed pattern across the body.

Squirrels are either right-handed or left-handed.

Squirrel Anatomy and Growth Although this may come as a surprise to most birders, there are other parts to a squirrel besides its eating/digestive system. Indeed, many lay people who study squirrels divide these mammals into two anatomically distinct systems: the part that eats, and the rest of the squirrel.

Perhaps the most prominent aspect of the squirrel is its tail. A squirrel's tail extends between eight and ten inches, as long as the squirrel is itself. A squirrel's tail is covered with a soft, fine fur; without this fur you would have a hard time telling the difference between a squirrel's tail and a rat's tail. The name squirrel is derived from the Greek words meaning "shade" and "tail." Squirrels' tails fulfill many purposes, including providing shade in the hot summer. Squirrels use their tails also for balance when leaping and climbing, for warmth in the winter when squirrels wrap their tails around them as they sleep, and to communicate with other squirrels. Because tails are so important, squirrels spend considerable time grooming them. Naturalist Alan Devoe wrote,

> The tail is to the squirrel, what vision is to the hawk or fleetness to a deer or wariness to a fox. He lives by it (quoted in *Our Animal Neighbors*, McGraw Hill, 1953).

Squirrels use their wide whiskers to determine whether the hole they're climbing into is large enough for them.

Squirrel coats have never faded from fashion. Men and women who own squirrel coats discover that the soft fur is pleasant to touch (assuming there are no live teeth attached to it), and very warm. Squirrels think so, too.

The gray squirrel isn't exclusively gray. The fur is a mixture of brown, gray and yellow on top, white and gray underneath; a squirrel's coloration changes as the seasons change. The tail appears silvered with dots of frosty white on the tips of the hair. There's no discernible difference between the appearance of male and female squirrels. The only way to tell which is which is to turn them upside down. It's not worth the effort.

The squirrel is a miracle of energy efficiency. Because squirrels do not hibernate, they must be prepared to brave the winter chills without the benefit of L.L. Bean. A squirrel's fur provides the first defense against the cold. Beneath the outer layer of fur is an underfur that gives squirrels added insulation and protects the skin. And beneath the skin is a layer of fat.

Squirrels grow slowly. When they are one day old, squirrels measure about four inches long, and are furless, pink and blind. They really do look like rats. When squirrels are two weeks old they've grown another one and a half inches, their skin has begun to darken, and—thank goodness—their hair has begun to appear. It is in the following week that a squirrel's incisors start to appear in its lower jaw. At week five squirrels open their eyes. They are now between nine and ten inches long, have developed their lower gnawing teeth and upper teeth, but still have no grinding teeth.

Grinding teeth appear in their sixth week of life. Around their seventh week squirrels have had their first taste of bark twigs, buds or leaves, but continue to derive most of their sustenance from their mother's milk. The baby squirrel's teeth make suckling at times uncomfortable for mother squirrels. It's around this time that squirrels first leave the nest, but many continue to be nursed until they are 12 weeks old. As Professor Vaun Flyger of the University of Maryland points out, "It takes longer to make a squirrel than other mammals." Those born in forests and New York City must forage for their food. Those who live in the suburbs where birdfeeders are plentiful have it made. Throughout the nursing stage squirrel mothers are not only attentive, but extremely protective of their young. People who try to inspect squirrel nests while the mother appears to be away are sometimes attacked by the mother squirrels who run to their childrens' defense. But once squirrels leave the nest for good, the squirrel family dissolves, and each squirrel is on its own.

Young squirrels are not automatically welcomed into a range. They must establish their own position—an estimated 10 percent of young squirrels are forced out of a range by more dominant ones. Ranges overlap.

Gray squirrels come in several pigments, gray, silver-gray, black and albino. In the East, black squirrels, also familiar in the Northwest, have been increasing in number over the past decade. They seem to prefer cities (they are numerous in Washington, D.C.) and do okay in the suburbs, but are rare in rural areas in the East. One theory explains this abundance of black squirrels by suggesting that city dwellers are especially protective of them. But the real reason behind the resurgence of black squirrels in cities remains unknown. According to squirrel-watcher Vaun Flyger, "We can only make wild guesses, but there seems to be an advantage to being a black squirrel here [in Washington, D.C.]. In rural areas black squirrels may not do as well because gray is better camouflage. Several hundred years ago black squirrels,

Prof. Vaun Flyger and his pet squirrel Fitzwilliam. (Don't try this stunt at home.)

which are more timid than grays, were more numerous, but destruction of forests probably gave grays an advantage over the decades—black squirrels were easier for predators to spot."

Squirrels thrive in urban areas, despite automobiles. One reason appears to be the prevalence of "urban islands," parks and other green spaces where squirrels have few predators. There's frequently an abundance of food, a "squirrel grocery" thanks to the carefree attitude of tourists and other do-gooders. The squirrels within these islands mate exclusively with each other, so you're likely to see a preponderance of black, gray, or even white squirrels in a park or similar area.

The Sex Life of Squirrels Female squirrels usually have two litters a year, each consisting of 3 or 4 infants. Once they've mated, the father squirrels usually desert their families and go off in search of food, other female squirrels, harassing birdfeeder owners—generally having a good time. Squirrels do not mate for life. You may think this is rather rotten, and that the male squirrels are sexist, but actually it's a good idea. Mating among different squirrels prevents inbreeding, ensures a stronger genetic pool, and helps the species survive. As another benefit to the species, females usually mate with older, more dominant males. The older males are better equipped to survive, and pass along those genes. After copulation, the male squirrel fills the female's vagina with a kind of waxy plug that prevents other males from copulating with her and locks the semen in.

Even though female squirrels bear the responsibility for rearing their young, life isn't so bad for females. First, they still get to raid birdfeeders. Second, females do invite and receive sex from younger males. Third, females control the sex act. Finally, they live longer than the males.

Smell plays a major role in mating among squirrels; males use it to locate females. Copulation can take place only when the female is in heat, called oestrus, which lasts only one day. Five days before oestrus occurs males begin to follow females. As many as twelve males will follow a female in a **mating bout**, or **chase**, during which the males will scream at and chase each other. One by one the less dominant males will go away in search of other partners. Dominant males expend considerable energy during this process. The winning male will follow the female through her home range, until she allows copulation.

Litters are spaced about thirteen to fourteen weeks apart, allowing females time to wean the babies. The gestation period is approximately 40 days. Peak birth times—during which 75 percent of the young are born—occur between the end of July and early August, and again in winter between late December and early January. This timetable is not fixed, but varies as weather and food conditions change.

You can use your knowledge about breeding to predict when the next crop of hungry squirrels will appear from their nest. Soon after young squirrels leave their nest you might want to temporarily cease feeding birds, or switch to thistle seed to encourage the squirrels to travel elsewhere.

Enemies of Squirrels The life of a squirrel in the wild is brief. Ten to twelve months, just long enough to see each season, is typical. In captivity they may live as long as 10 to 15 years; one such squirrel lived long enough to die of prostate cancer.

Squirrels have several enemies. But birders aren't among them. Squirrels may run away from you when you come at them flailing your arms and screaming, but they learn that you aren't going to hurt them because they know you don't want a dead squirrel in your yard. At window feeders squirrels discover that glass is a perfect protection and no matter how loudly you pound the glass you're not going to stick your arm through it.

Some squirrel "enemies" such as woodpeckers merely annoy squirrels. According to *Animals of the World*,

> . . . the Gray Squirrel is not the only claimant for the nuts; the Red Squirrel and the red-headed woodpeckers demand the lion's share. The birds seem to think that these nuts are exclusively their property, and vigorously do they protest if a Squirrel appears. One determined woodpecker will sometimes send a Gray Squirrel scampering after a few moments, for the blows from that long sharp bill of his are severe. The Squirrels, being the earlier risers, are often feasting when the birds appear, but they beat a hasty retreat before these tri-colored warriors (Garden City Publishing Co., 1941, p. 165).

Crows, blue jays and mockingbirds are other feathered friends who will harass squirrels.

But squirrels have too many deadly enemies in urban, rural, and suburban areas. Hunters kill roughly 40 million squirrels each year in the eastern part of the United States. And although that doesn't make a significant dent in the American squirrel population, it's something squirrels aren't crazy about. A greater danger to squirrels is automobiles. A familiar scene: a squirrel runs exactly half way across a road as a car approaches. The driver accelerates. The squirrel turns around and runs back. Bam: flattened fauna. It's not entirely clear why squirrels do this, and none of American's leading squirrel experts satisfactorily explain the phenomenon. However, the *Dick E. Bird News* offers this reasoning:

> Their tail scurries across the ground at around 10 mph and jumps from tree branch to tree branch pushing their bodies ahead of it. Talk about being pushed around all the time. One big problem is that quite often a squirrel will get out into the middle of the road when a car is coming. When this happens the tail usually wants to go one way and the body wants to go another. But the time they get their differences worked out, it's often too late.

The worst kind of streets are those with median dividers. In those cities with concrete dividers, such as Boston, life is even harder. "You make it across the first four lanes of traffic, and you're still stuck," said Dr. Thomas French, a zoologist at the Massachusetts Division of Fisheries and Wildlife.

Predators are a problem for squirrels. These predators include cats, dogs, snakes, weasels, ferrets, red-tailed hawks, barred owls, foxes, raccoons, boys with B B guns, and even largemouth bass (one was found with squirrel remains inside.) Predators pose different threats to squirrels, causing squirrels to react differently in each case. Dogs, cats, barred owls, and hawks will attack and dine on squirrels of all ages. A squirrel that is out in the open— in a field not near a tree—is essentially squirrel meat when chased by one of these. Sharp as a squirrel's claws are, squirrels are no match for these creatures. A squirrel's best defense, and sometimes its only defense, is hiding in trees. Just about everyone who has watched squirrels has noticed their ability to hide from their enemies by lying flat against the opposite side of a tree. As the enemy moves, the squirrel moves.

Snakes and raccoons enjoy the taste of young squirrels, but tend to leave the larger ones alone. These predators can enter squirrels' burrows.

When confronted by a dog, cat, or predatory bird, squirrels will run as quickly as they can to the nearest burrow or tree, observe the predator, and retreat only when approached. Squirrels will often stand their ground against weasels, ferrets and snakes—squirrels will confront them and even harass them.

When threatened, squirrels often chatter, scold, and try to warn other squirrels.

Becoming dinner isn't the only danger that squirrels face. By far their greatest enemy is malnutrition. Not enough food kills the majority of squirrels in the wild, either directly or by making them susceptible to disease. Squirrels live in a harsh environment. Babies born in the summer may face their first winter storm when they are only fifteen weeks old—it's hard to gather food in that kind of weather.

Sarcoptic mange claims a large percentage of squirrels in winter. Caused by mites, this disease strikes underfed squirrels causing them to lose their fur. In the summer mites are only a nuisance for squirrels—all they have to do is scratch—but in the winter fur loss is deadly.

The warble fly begins to bug squirrels in August and September, causing swellings behind the forelegs and on the shoulders. These lumps occur where the warble fly has deposited its larvae. Squirrels infested with the warble fly often have blood oozing from lumps on their skin.

Various nematode worms and cysts plague squirrels as well. Some squirrels have been found with over 100 worms in them, a condition squirrels aren't enthusiastic about.

Social Activities　For all their running around, squirrels don't go very far. (Why should they with people like you who graciously feed them?) A squirrel's range is between 1 and 7 acres. The home range of males is twice as large as the range of females, possibly because males are more persnickety than females about what they eat. Females are happy with leaves and berries, while males really want those nuts. The range of males increases during breeding seasons, which enhances the chances of getting a mate. Territoriality doesn't seem to be a trait of gray squirrels. They roam freely within their home range, pretty much ignoring other squirrels except under certain circumstances. Female squirrels will defend their nests. When males vie for dominance over females they yell and harass each other. At birdfeeders both male and female grays will argue over who has rights to the feeder first. Arguing squirrels rarely come into contact (their chisel-sharp teeth are reserved for **you**). Instead squirrels like to scream and shake their tails at one another. (A few species of squirrels do exercise territoriality. Fortunately none of these species is interested in birdseed. Could you imagine one squirrel defending a feeder from all other squirrels?) While home ranges overlap, newcomers to a particular range may be met with aggression.

Some mornings you may be awakened by the sweet songs of birds. Other times you may bolt upright after hearing the shrill, piercing sound that goes something like **cheeoo eeeeoooo**. That's squirrel talk. What are they saying? They must be doing something other than deliberately trying to deprive you of sleep. Squirrels are unusually vocal animals and actually use their voices to communicate. There are no direct relationships between particular sounds and what squirrels are trying to say; in other words, squirrels have no vocabulary or language as we understand it. As Donald H. Owings and David Hennessy put it in their scholarly article, "The Importance of Variation in Sciurid Visual and Vocal Communication," squirrel "calling is not structurally unitary but varies at multiple levels and correlates with variation in calling situations" (*The Biology of Ground-Dwelling Squirrels*, Jan O. Murie and Gail Michener, eds, University of Nebraska Press, 1984).

In other words, squirrel sounds do not have meaning in isolation from the conditions they are in. Even calls under the same circumstance may mean different things to different squirrels. For example, when a snake is in the vicinity, adult squirrels may be warning other squirrels with their call, while young squirrels may be recruiting help. Squirrels use their calls and tail signals to alert other squirrels and to intimidate their adversaries, including other squirrels. Squirrels continue to call after the danger appears to have passed, possibly because they know that the danger may persist beyond their line of sight and other squirrels may be in jeopardy: through their calls squirrels exhibit a strong determination to preserve their species.

How the squirrel uses its tail is not entirely understood. Unlike a squirrel's call, tail movements are not restricted by the amount of air a squirrel can manipulate. Tail movements can be held for a long time and varied within that time, and a squirrel uses this motion for many of the same purposes as their calls. However, tail motion also helps a squirrel balance, and at times may be used simultaneously for balance and signalling.

Mr. Squirrel trying out for a part in the high-wire act.

Squirrels also use smell to communicate. Marking the underside of branches with urine so that the smell isn't washed off by rain, and anal dragging are two common forms of scent marking.

Although you may see gray squirrels chase each other, especially the males around mating times, squirrels are cordial animals. This trait is particularly noticeable in their nests. According to Vaun Flyger, "Males and immature females will sleep together. I've seen as many as six or seven squirrel in one nest." Mature females are not included in this crowd: it would become sexually confusing if they slept in the same nest as several males. "Mature females become loners," says Vaun Flyger.

There are four kinds of squirrel nests. Both males and females help build nests. The one most commonly seen by humans is the **drey**, or winter nest. They are roughly 12 to 16 inches in diameter, waterproof, and made of twigs on the outside, and moss, bark, fur, feathers, lichen, and leaves on the inside. Winter dreys take one to three days to construct and are strong enough to withstand harsh winds. They are never built too low where predators can reach them, nor too high where the winds are more severe. Summer dreys are smaller and more fragile, consisting of twigs and leaves.

Squirrels also live in cavities of trees, called tree dens. These cavities are created by woodpeckers or branches that have fallen away. Finally, squirrels sometimes build their nests in holes in the ground, which can provide considerable insulation against the cold.

The hierarchy that is manifest in squirrel mating behavior is also apparent in day-to-day life, and is strictly adhered to. Less dominant squirrels defer to the older, larger, and more assertive males, not only during mating, but at food sources. Dominant squirrels eat first. Squirrels yell, wave their tails, and chase each other, but as I mentioned earlier, there is very little physical contact between them. They know who is dominant and who is subordinate. This hierarchy, Professor Flyger speculates, helps keep squirrels from fighting one another.

Several times in this chapter I've made references to squirrel behavior that helps preserve the species, behavior that can sometimes be described as altruistic. This behavior includes:

1. Burying nuts for all squirrels in the range.
2. Males mating with various females to prevent genetic inbreeding.
3. Sleeping together to preserve body heat.
4. Warning other squirrels of danger.

The Expert Squirrel Watcher   There was one name that continued to crop up in my reading and interviews about squirrels: Dr. Vaun Flyger. In *The World of the Gray Squirrel* there was Vaun Flyger and his studies of squirrels. In an article entitled "Climactic Influences on Life-History Tactics and Behavior [of Squirrels]," Vaun Flyger appeared again. He wrote a seminal article entitled "Movement and Home Range of the Gray Squirrel." Who is Vaun Flyger? He has written extensively on the nesting behavior of squirrels and their population dynamics. How did he become one of the foremost experts on gray squirrels? What is a squirrel expert like? I decided to visit Vaun Flyger to find out.

Vaun Flyger looks the way you'd expect the movie character Indiana Jones, played by Harrison Ford, to look in 20 years or so. A little thicker around the middle than he once was, a little less hair, and a walk that is less speedy than it once was, but still strong. He has a definite outdoors look to him: thick hands, weathered skin, a pleasantly rough face—the marks of a man who has spent much of his time outdoors and does plenty of physical work. His eyes appear sharp, as if they are practiced in spotting objects that most people wouldn't see. He appears jovial and confident, an enviable combination.

Vaun Flyger lives in Silver Spring, Maryland, a suburb of Washington, D.C. (squirrel capital of America) which is near the University of Maryland, where he teaches about mammals. The drive takes about 45 minutes from downtown Washington, passing mostly highway and convenience stores, until you near Vaun Flyger's house. As you turn into the semi-paved road that leads to his home, you begin to think that not too far from here is the perfect location for someone who has made his career the study of mammals.

Prof. Flyger seated me in one of the many comfortable, oversized chairs in his house and began to tell me about squirrels. I didn't need to ask many questions; a simple mention of the word squirrel and he was off talking.

Vaun Flyger's first academic encounter with squirrels came when he was asked to do a study in Maryland on whether the length of the hunting season affected the squirrel population. At the time Maryland had a short hunting season. Flyger recommended that the season's length be extended: although 40-50 million squirrels are killed by hunters in the Eastern part of the United States each year (1/2 million in Maryland alone), "no one has been able to demonstrate that hunting has reduced the population at all." One of the reasons for that is "a hunter sees only 1/6 of the squirrels that are out there. We know this because we put radio transmitters on squirrels."

During this project, Prof. Flyger found that "squirrels were convenient animals to study."

It was at this point that I asked Dr. Flyger, "Have you ever been bitten?" That's kind of a rhetorical question, of course, for a man who studies squirrels, but I had to ask. Flyger responded, "Oh yes. But it's not too bad, it's a relative thing. After all, I used to work with polar bears."

This question prompted Vaun Flyger to begin talking about the kinds of things that squirrels eat. "They eat many different things," he said. "Most people don't realize that squirrels eat fungi and tree bark, which are just about as important to squirrels as nuts. Squirrels dig for truffle-like mushrooms." Now you know who's to blame for the outrageous price of truffles, I thought, as Flyger continued. "Nineteen eighty-eight's going to be a bad year for squirrels, because we had a bad acorn crop last fall," he said, sounding slightly solemn. "The fall of 1985 was a great acorn crop for squirrels. But this last fall there was the seventeen year locust and squirrels were filling up on cicadas. Breeding reflects the amount of food there is for squirrels, so there was a bumper crop of young. We came into the fall of 1987 with a lot more squirrels than we should have." Flyger's silence said the rest: a lot of squirrels died over the winter.

But this was not the worst loss because of an acorn shortage. "Between 1953 and 1954, 95 percent of the squirrels disappeared."

The squirrel's day is not as hectic as it may appear from watching them attack feeders and run up and down trees. "A squirrel spends a large part of its day just snoozing," Vaun Flyger said, changing the subject. "When the weather is warm, he just stretches out on the branches and sleeps. On a typical August or September day a squirrel will spend a lot of the day eating and building up fat." Listening to Professor Flyger, I began to feel that squirrels were a lot more like people than I had ever thought. He continued, "In winter they don't eat as much. They're not as active— they get up later and go to sleep earlier."

Professor Flyger reinforced the notion that squirrels are a disciplined lot. "Chuck chuck chuck" is the alarm call of squirrels. When they do that and start waving their tails, they're excited about something. It tells other squirrels that they should be on the alert. Other squirrels take notice and run half way up a tree, watch, and wait."

By making this alarm call, a squirrel may be drawing the attention of predators away from other squirrels, toward itself. If this is true, then this is an example of highly altruistic behavior.

Vaun Flyger has also spent considerable time studying the red squirrel, which "sings like a bird." He mentioned this because the interaction between grays and reds shows that gray squirrels are not so omnipotent after all. Smaller than the gray squirrel, the red is territorial. Although grays bury their nuts communally, red squirrels defend their nuts. So what happens when the two subspecies come into contact? "The red treats grays like a red and will chase them. Even though the grays are larger, they usually defer to the reds." (But if you're thinking about importing red squirrels to your yard, be forewarned, reds like feeder foods, too.)

I asked Vaun Flyger about protecting your feeder from squirrels. I asked which is the most squirrel-proof feeder. He mentioned a couple of feeders but then pointed out perhaps the best way to outwit them: "the best way to cure the problem is to treat a squirrel like a chicken." "Like a chicken?" I asked. "Yes," he continued. "Any recipe that works for chicken will work for squirrel. And they're low in cholesterol."

Vaun Flyger explained some more. The ability of any particular area to support squirrels is limited. That's called the "carrying capacity." "When you move a squirrel to a new area"—many birders trap squirrels and ship their problem elsewhere—"it increases the amount of stress on the carrying capacity in that range because the squirrels moved there increase the number of squirrels in the range. Either the new squirrels or the less dominant squirrels have to leave—or die. I discovered this by dyeing transported squirrels purple." That's why "it's better to trap and eat squirrels than move them." Then he added, "depending on the game laws."

After we talked for a while at Prof. Flyger's indoor-outdoor house, he gave me a tour of the grounds. It's difficult not to feel spirited by the surrounding acres of unspoiled woods, especially when you were on a highway only minutes before. But the woods aren't entirely untouched; there are about a dozen feeders, nesting boxes and other contraptions. The first place Flyger brought me to was a large cage about a hundred feet behind his house. The cage was big enough to hold several people. There he introduced me to Fitzwilliam, Flyger's pet squirrel. Fitzwilliam is a fox squirrel, which at first glance looks like a gray, but is actually a little larger, has a rounder face, sort of like a fox, and a reddish-brown hue. I'd never seen a squirrel as a pet before, although I'd heard stories about people who kept them inside in order to lower the value of their house to keep their tax assessment down. Fitzwilliam, adopted from one of Vaun Flyger's former students who had been studying him, stays in his cage all the time; but this doesn't dampen the squirrel's spirits. Without hesitating, Flyger opened Fitzwilliam's cage and stepped inside. I had a different reaction: I adjusted my telephoto lens and stepped back. But as soon as Professor Flyger was inside, Fitzwilliam jumped on his arm and ran over his shoulders, just like a kitten. Later when the squirrel expert played with Fitzwilliam by rubbing his nose, Fitzwilliam played back by batting Flyger with his paw—playfully. Vaun Flyger discovered how good a squirrel's memory can be by watching Fitzwilliam: when Flyger returns from a trip Fitzwilliam runs and jumps because he's glad to see his friend.

Flyger then showed me an L-shaped apparatus he uses to feed squirrels that was originally designed in Great Britain to poison squirrels. He fills the L-tube with corn. "The squirrels eat the germ of the corn and the birds eat the rest." More than anything else I saw that morning, this squirrel feeder satisfies Vaun Flyger's sense of total ecological utility. While we were standing by the squirrel feeder a squirrel yelled at us from a nearby tree. "He's mad because we're at his feeder," Flyger pointed out.

But lest you think that Vaun Flyger is in the other camp (you know, the pro-squirrel side), I should add that his birdfeeders are prominent and popular. The best way to describe Prof. Flyger is to say he is an unbiased observer.

The size of a squirrel's litter is positively correlated with latitude. The warmer the climate the greater the number of litters produced each year by squirrels.

Despite their "tameness" squirrels are difficult to breed in captivity. Their elaborate courtship ritual involving several males chasing a female is an essential prerequisite to mating.

Mass migrations of squirrels have been reported. In 1882 an estimated 250,000 squirrels migrated across Ohio.

4

The Unbearable Persistence of Squirrel Appetites

"Squirrels consider bird feeders as special challenges."

New York Times

It was during that indefinite time between late winter and early spring when, despite the fickleness of the weather, flowers are appearing, that my friend Randy Rieland discovered that I was writing a book about outwitting squirrels. Randy said he watched the crocuses pop up in his yard one afternoon and disappear the following afternoon. Randy suspected a culprit. "Do squirrels eat crocuses?" he asked.

"They do," I replied. "They eat the buds and bulbs from many flowers. It's something they look forward to all winter long. They also like tulips."

Squirrels have a way of creating maximum annoyance in gardens. You never know what they're going to do. Henry Mitchell, a writer for the *Washington Post*, reported, "[F]or two years they made surgical slanting cuts on some Ilam and Exbury azaleas as the buds began to swell, just before blooming season. I had heard squirrels sometimes like to eat the resinous buds, so I covered them with nylon stocking. It was then that the squirrels cut the stems and carried off the buds in their stockings."

While most bird feeders worry about pilferage of seed, other outdoor hobbyists are devastated by squirrels, too. The squirrel is the nemesis of the gardener. A hungry squirrel—is there any other kind?—will devour any flower-like growth in sight. They're particularly tempted by buds, but they will eat everything save for the stem. Having squirrels in your yard when the first flowers come up is like having a lawnmower run amok. Mary McGrory pointed out that if you feed birds and have a garden, you're in lots of trouble. "They do vindictive landscaping."

This could happen to any feeder: when a squirrel can't get into a feeder, it simply takes it down. Notice how fat the squirrel in this photograph is.

Squirrel appetites extend into our national parks. In 1983 the National Park Service conducted a census of squirrels in Lafayette Park, across the street from The White House. Park spokesman Duncan Morrow suspected that many squirrels were subsidized by White House staffers. "There are a number of White House staff people who show up pretty regularly with stuff they feed the squirrels."

The park is the nation's most popular spot for demonstrations. Still, a Park Service spokesman said, "There is not much damage to the park from demonstrators. The biggest damage we get is from squirrels eating the bulbs of plants."

Bird, squirrel, and garden lover Heather Perram has a solution for vindictive gardeners. She said that if you plant mothballs around your flowers the squirrels will leave them alone.

Biologist Roger Swain, science editor of *Horticulture Magazine,* is keenly aware of the squirrel problem. Swain, who wrote his doctoral dissertation about tropical ants, has spent countless hours trying to figure out ways to outwit squirrels from a gardener's point of view. (The shift from studying ants to what he now does was natural, he said. "I just added a **p** and an **l**.") His opinions are blunt. "The best thing to do is to get rid of squirrels. They're terrible for plants. Squirrels eat fruit and buds just as they're coming out.

"I was once giving a lecture in which I said you should get rid of them. Unfortunately there was an officer from the humane society in the audience who said he just gave a $250 ticket to someone for killing a squirrel. I'd gladly pay the bail of that person."

Perhaps birders and gardeners should join forces to outwit squirrels, I said. Horticulturalists have discovered how hard it is to thwart squirrels, especially because you can't hang plants in the air as you can with feeders. "The one thing you can't do is educate a squirrel through terror. People, who are higher up on the food chain, remember terror. But when you are squirrel size you're scared witless many times a day." Their whole day involves fear, said Swain. "To survive as a squirrel you must be able to forget the last time you were scared." Fear is not imprinted into a squirrel's memory. "If a squirrel or woodchuck remembered fear it would die of fright, it's scared too many times." Swain offered this analogy: "A short order cook can only succeed by forgetting the last thing he cooked."

In the following essay, Roger Swain elaborates another side of the squirrel problem.

THE SQUIRREL AND THE FRUITCAKE

Pecans are a choice ingredient of both fruitcake and squirrels. Some ten million pounds are incorporated annually into each. In fruitcake, pecans improve the color, texture, and taste, for the nuts offset the darkness, gumminess, and molasses flavor of the candied fruit. In squirrels, the nuts are vital. A diet of pecans, with their 70 percent oil content, is responsible for a higher birthrate, increased survival of the young, reduced emigration, and longer life for adults. In short, more squirrels.

With the quality of both squirrels and fruitcakes dependent on the seeds of *Carya illinoinenis,* there has always been competition for the nuts.

From the point of view of the nut grower, squirrels make off with far too many pecans. Climbing into the trees, the squirrels begin to feed on the nuts even before they are ripe and later remove the largest and finest nuts from the opening shucks. Nuts that have fallen are picked up off the ground. In all, a single squirrel may make off with fifty pounds of pecans in a four-month period. Some of these nuts are eaten on the spot; others are carried up to a hundred feet away and cached singly in shallow holes dug in the ground.

From the squirrel's point of view, the human is far too successful at usurping the harvest. Nut trees that have been planted far away from adjoining forest are often surrounded by a dangerous expanse of closely mown ground; crossing this open ground means exposure to hawks, foxes, dogs, and other squirrel eaters. Reaching the grove may provide little sanctuary: guns and traps baited with pecans constitute another, greater hazard. If someone has protected the trees with eighteen-inch-wide bands of aluminum flashing tied around the trunks, the trees are unclimbable anyway. Scarcely any nuts are on the ground until they are knocked or shaken from the trees by the harvesters, and when that happens the grove is filled with people. For a squirrel whose ancestors harvested pecans long before humans appeared on this continent, this is an unpleasant development.

"The Squirrel and the Fruitcake" first appeared in *Horticulture Magazine* and then in Roger Swain's *Earthly Pleasures* (Penguin Books, 1981). It is reproduced here by kind permission of the author.

The displeasure that humans and squirrels may share at having to divide up the pecan crop is compounded by the periodic disappearance of pecans from a tree altogether. The nonproduction of nuts is a periodic occurrence, especially in the year following a heavy harvest. A heavy crop will exhaust the tree's supply of stored carbohydrates, and the ripening of so many nuts prevents the tree from storing enough carbohydrates to bear the following year. Pecan growers refer to this as "alternate bearing" and determinedly try to prevent it through breeding, high fertilization, and careful spacing and pruning of trees to promote additional photosynthesis. As a further strategy, growers often plant four or five pecan cultivars in a single grove so that some of the trees will be bearing each year.

While growers and squirrels may both consider a year without pecans to be a crop failure, from the point of view of the pecan tree itself, such a year is not a failure at all. Pecans are reproductive units intended to increase the population of pecan trees, not squirrels. A given pecan tree might fruit every year, but then there would always be the same number of squirrels, pecan fed and ready to consume all of the crop once again. On the other hand, a pecan tree that saved up its carbohydrates for several years would not be feeding squirrels. There might be fewer squirrels in the absence of pecans, and when the tree did fruit, producing a much larger crop because of its stores of carbohydrates, the reduced squirrel population might be unable to consume all of the nuts. Some pecans would escape to become pecan trees.

For a pecan tree to effectively elude nut predators by concentrating its nut production into one year, all the trees in the vicinity must bear nuts the same year. Otherwise the predators will simply feed on the nuts of one tree one year and the nuts of another the next. This synchronization is not as improbable as it sounds. There already exists remarkable synchronization among nut trees, even in forests containing many species. Measurements on the amount of hickory nuts, acorns, beechnuts, and other seeds in a forest in southeastern Ohio from year to year showed a range of 35 to 220 pounds per acre.

Whether in a forest or a grove, the concentration of nut production into only a few years results in lean years, which to both squirrels and pecan growers are entirely unwelcome. But from the point of view of the pecan tree, nonproduction means that the tree is not losing its nuts to predators. The pecan tree can't give up fruiting altogether, because eventually the tree must reproduce itself. The tree has simply evolved a specific behavior, in the form of irregular fruiting, that serves at least partially to prevent the total destruction of the nut crop by squirrels and other predators.

Ecologists and evolutionary biologists term this behavior "predator satiation." There are some extremely dramatic examples among plants. The bamboo *Phyllostachys bambusoides,* for example, fruits only every 120 years, with all the plants doing so at once. Among nut trees the interval is much less, usually a year or two between seed crops, but the bitternut (*Carya cordiformis*) has a three-to-five-year interval and the white oak (*Quercus alba*) a four-to-ten-year interval. The European beech (*Fagus sylvatica*) accumulates starch in the parenchyma of the sapwood for about eight years. It is then virtually completely incorporated into a single seed crop and then storage is resumed.

While the pecan trees have evolved a way to assure the survival of some of their nuts, they also have become dependent on squirrels to distribute and plant those same nuts. The thickness of the shell of wild pecans is largely a result of selection by squirrels. Pecans whose shells are too thick or too hard to be pierced by squirrel teeth will not be collected, and the trees producing these nuts will remain unpropagated. Pecans whose shells are too thin are likely to be eaten much too readily rather than buried in the ground where a small percentage will remain to germinate.

With the arrival of modern agriculture, the pecan is no longer dependent on the squirrel for propagation. Seedlings are grown in nurseries and transplanted into groves. Careful breeding and improved cultural practices have greatly improved the pecan tree. New cultivars bear early, annually, and prolifically. Nuts are larger, have thinner shells, and are well filled. The only situation that hasn't improved is the problem with squirrels.

The annual loss of pecans to squirrels is difficult to compute. In Georgia alone, an estimated ten million pounds of pecans are eaten by predators, including crows, blackbirds, and jays as well as squirrels. If we assume that squirrels account for one-third of this amount and, further, that Georgia produces roughly one-third of the nation's pecans, then we arrive at an annual nationwide loss to squirrels of ten million pounds of pecans a year.

Boxcar figures are not very useful and indeed they tend to obscure the much greater losses experienced by certain pecan growers. Especially in years of a small harvest, the loss may amount to more than 50 percent. In such "short crop" years, every nut on a tree may be stolen. One expert remarked sardonically that, in some areas of Georgia, pecans are borderline between a cash crop and wildlife feed.

Some people, especially those who have just lost a sizable portion of their pecan crop, would be in favor of exterminating squirrels. Because attempts to exterminate them would almost certainly fail, current efforts are focused on reducing the numbers of squirrels by hunting and trapping or keeping them away with noisemakers, metal barriers around trunks, or fine-wire fences reinforced with electricity.

From what we have learned of the behavior of squirrels and pecan trees, an alternative squirrel-control method suggests itself. Since we have undertaken to improve the pecan tree through artificial breeding and selection, why not produce a squirrel-proof pecan? Whether or not the effort of selecting for squirrel resistance is economically feasible remains to be determined, but such a cultivar is certainly possible. This hypothetical squirrel-proof pecan cultivar would have the following two characteristics, traits the opposite of those being favored by current selection practices.

1. The cultivar would fruit only after long intervals of time, five to ten years if possible, with little or no nut production in intervening years. With all the adjoining trees fruiting at the same time, there would be a single enormous crop that would satiate squirrels and other predators.

2. Nuts of the cultivar would have a very thick shell, too thick for squirrels to gnaw through easily. If the costs in energy of breaking into a nut exceed the nutritive value of the nutmeat therein, the squirrels will turn to other foods. Thicker-shelled pecans would prompt squirrels to seek more accessible nutrition.

Groves of this new pecan should still be isolated from other food sources of squirrels to make it difficult for squirrels to move into a fruiting grove. Home gardeners who might have to plant these trees close to an adjoining squirrel habitat would probably benefit more from the thicker-shelled feature than from the concentrated bearing. On the other hand, concentrated bearing would offer both the home gardener and the commercial grower considerable relief from such insect pests as the pecan weevil and the hickory shuckworm. These pecan pests are much more dependent on pecans for survival and their populations will crash more dramatically than squirrels in the nonbearing years.

A number of objections to squirrel-proof pecans come immediately to mind and must be addressed. Will pecan trees that fruit only once a decade mean nine years of nutless fruitcakes? Absolutely not. Different parts of the country could be on different schedules with one grove bearing this year, another the next. It would only be necessary to establish nut-free zones between unsynchronized groves of pecans. A second solution is to store pecans between harvests. Fifty years ago pecan storage had not progressed beyond that achieved by squirrels. Pecans could be kept fresh during the cool winter months, but as soon as spring warmth arrived, the nuts became stale and rancid. Since then, however, it has been shown that in controlled cold storage, pecans can be kept for eight years with no loss in color, flavor, or texture of the shelled pecans. A long hiatus between harvests will deprive only the squirrels, not the fruitcakes.

A second objection will come from fanciers of paper-shelled pecans, those nuts that are easily shelled by hand. However, less than 10 percent of the pecan crop each year is sold to consumers in the shell. The remaining 90 percent is machine shelled. There is no reason why the established cultivars could not continue to provide nuts for the in-shell market. The new thicker-shelled cultivar would simply require a stronger machine.

Finally, conservationists concerned about preserving the squirrel population need not be alarmed. Squirrels have sufficient quantities of food available to them in the form of a host of wild edibles that they face no danger of extinction.

This highly hypothetical proposal for a squirrel-proof pecan is illustrative of a different approach to crop plant design. In breeding plants to conform to our commercial needs, we tend to ignore their peculiar characteristics, traits that have evolved during centuries of selective pressure, in this case the fruiting cycles of nut trees. More efforts should be directed at reexamining the biology of wild crop plants for clues to their natural resistance to pests and disease. In some instances we may have overlooked a trait, and in the process of artificial selection, we may have exacerbated a problem rather than alleviated it. Domestication of plants has removed some ecological constraints, such as a need for natural propagation. In seeking means to meet existing pressures, we may be able to select more vigorously for a certain trait than previous ecological constraints would allow. Most trees fruit more often than once a century because there is too much danger of their being blow down or burned up before they reproduce. Having undertaken to propagate pecan trees ourselves, we can select for longer rather than shorter intervals between harvests and for nuts with heavier shells. This may ultimately prove to be an easier way to reduce nut losses than trying to exterminate the predators. With new pecan cultivars, we could have our fruitcake and squirrels, too.

Ground squirrels consume 24 ounces of nuts a week. They can eat 3 ounces at a sitting.

5

Rating the Feeders

Which feeder to buy? Which will attract the most birds? Which will attract the kind of birds you covet? Which are easiest to fill, and which are pains in the neck to fill? Which will fend off squirrels? This chapter, Rating the Feeders, answers these irksome questions, and gives advice on how to select the best feeder for your needs.

Squirrel-Proof or Squirrel Resistant? Or have you merely created a diner for squirrels? Dozens of different birdfeeders are on the market, and not all of them are going to offer the kind of squirrel-resistance you want. Selecting the appropriate feeder is often a matter of trial and error: squirrels **try** to break into your feeder and then you notice your **error** in buying that feeder.

There's no perfect feeder. Although a couple are highly squirrel-resistant—especially the GSP, Mandarin, and Looker SPF Feeder—and others can be made squirrel-resistant with the use of baffles, grease and other barriers, there is no feeder that is squirrel-proof all the time. These critters are capable seed stealers. Even when they can't leap into a feeder, squirrels can claw a few seeds out, shake seed to the ground, knock the feeder to the ground and feast on the booty, or bite their way through.

Squirrel-resistance varies, too, depending on how you place your feeder. Certain feeders, for example, are squirrel-resistant when placed on top of a pole, but lose their resistance when hung from a tree. I prefer the expression squirrel-resistant to squirrel-proof. Squirrel-proof exists only in an idealized state. Peggy Robin, a Washington, D.C. bird feeder, points out that whether a feeder is squirrel-resistant or squirrel-proof is a state of mind. If you can't tolerate squirrels at all, there's no such thing as a squirrel-proof feeder.

Some Strategies for Making Feeders Squirrel-Resistant

If a feeder isn't as squirrel-resistant as you would like, attempt some home-brewed remedies. Take the initiative! Don't cower to a tiny animal! Show those squirrels who's boss! Turn your anger into a positive force! There are plenty of things you can do besides yelling and throwing frisbees at the squirrels. For example, if your feeder is hanging from a tree that's not near any other tree, place a sheet metal skirt around the tree to prevent squirrels from climbing up. Maybe the hanging chain the feeder came with isn't long enough—lengthen it with coated, copper wire. Put vaseline on the wire once a month if that helps. Perhaps the feeder needs a baffle or two, or the baffle the feeder came with isn't large enough. If the feeder is too close to a tree, move it further out on the branch. The cardinal rule is a feeder can't become squirrel-proof if it's in a place where squirrels can get to it. (Chapter 6 discusses anti-squirrel devices you can buy and build.)

Certain locations should be avoided, such as tree branches, according to Marlene Couture of the Duncraft Company in Penacook, New Hampshire. "We try to tell people not to hang feeders from a tree. It's the worst place possible, but people put it there because it's the only place they can see them. No matter what you do, no matter what baffles you use, the feeder is right there under the squirrel's nose. It's like hanging lunch in front of them. Eventually they will get to it. And if they can't get to it, they'll knock it down." If you do hang your feeder from a tree, there are certain precautions that may help. Place the feeder as far out on the branch as possible, use a wire instead of a chain because the wire is "slicker." Baffle the feeder. If you can't hang the feeder far out on a limb because the tree limb is too fragile to support a feeder at its end, use a narrow tube feeder that squirrels won't be able to reach from the tree trunk.

Couture recommends poles and brackets instead of hanging feeders from trees—her ideal place is on top of a pole with a squirrel guard baffle beneath. Keep the pole as far away from trees and fences as possible. Failing that, she suggests stringing a heavy fishing line or wire between two trees and hanging the feeder from the line, along with some devices to discourage squirrels from walking along the line.

Be imaginative when it comes to where you put your feeder.

There's More to a Feeder Than Squirrel-Resistance Squirrel-resistance isn't the only criteron that you may have for a feeder. Another important consideration is how easily you can view the birds. Bird visibility doesn't depend just on the kind of feeder, either: how you position it is crucial. The GSP feeder, one of the few that could be called squirrel-proof, sometimes gives a good view of birds, and sometimes offers a lousy view as it rotates. Wooden hanging feeders only let you view the birds that are on your side of the feeder because wood is opaque. When you're buying a new feeder, think about where you're going to put it *and where you're going to watch it from.* It's no fun to feed birds you can't watch.

You can improve the visibility of birds by blocking those openings on the opposite side from where you view the feeder, which will encourage birds to flutter around to the side where you want them. You may block particular openings to deter squirrels as well. If the feeder's on a chain that rotates, replace the chain with a metal rod. (Metal rods are easier to grease than chains, too.) After a while baffles can become dirty and scratched; clean them or replace them.

Seed capacity is crucial, too. You don't—repeat don't!—want to fill your feeder every day, so tiny feeders are out. If your yard sports several feeders or if you're going to be outside frequently, then it's okay to have a small capacity feeder. But nothing discourages feeding birds more than filling a feeder daily. Window feeders have notoriously small capacities, but they are an exception to this rule because you can usually fill them from inside. I suggest a quart as an absolute minimum for a non-window feeder; the gallon-plus feeders are the smartest buy. If your feeder is in a hard to reach location then seed capacity may the most important criterion in your choice of feeders.

However, having too large a feeder isn't good either. If the seed in your feeder isn't consumed within a week or two, consider switching to a smaller capacity feeder. The longer seed sits in a feeder the more likely it is to rot and becomes disease-ridden. There's a trade-off between convenience and serving safe seed. More on this later.

Ease of refilling goes hand in hand with seed capacity. The most annoying feeders are those with tiny seed capacities and those that are difficult to fill. Ideally you just want to pour the seed in, as most window feeders allow; the second best option is to lift a light lid and pour the seed. Many feeders have caps that must be pulled or pried off—a real pain. Besides, eventually these caps get lost. Beware of feeders that need two hands to hold the seed cavity open, or that require a *strong* arm to do the trick. The larger the opening, the better, too. The Mandarin, one of the best designed feeders, has an opening for seed that is so large you could pour a bucket of seed in. Watch out, also, for feeders where you must tilt the seed disperser at a specific angle in order to get the seed in. Ask yourself: will I be able to fill the feeder easily from where I am going to put it?

Another important question is what the feeder looks like. Every time you peer into your yard you're going to see that feeder, so you had better be certain that you like the way it's designed. A feeder that looks unpleasant in the store will look even worse when you bring it home. Birds couldn't care less about a feeder's construction; a dogfood bowl with sunflower seed in it would make them happy. Most feeders sold in catalogs are fairly ordinary. Others are engineered to resemble swiss cottages and are usually made of clear, sturdy plastic, which may become muddy-looking over time.

For the most artistically demanding birders, a number of craftspeople are putting art and imagination to the design of bird-feeders. Richard Clarke, who runs The Bird House in Portland, Oregon, handcrafts his feeders. Of the dozens of designs that are available, you should be able to find the one that suits your taste. (One word of caution: squirrels will eat through feeders to get at seed, so if you buy a house-beautiful feeder, make certain that squirrels either can't get to it, or if they can,they can reach the seed without having to make a hole in your feeder.)

One last consideration is a feeder's weather-resistance. Wet seed quickly becomes covered with dangerous mold. Rain, snow, and wind affect feeders differently. A stiff wind can empty some feeders as quickly as a family of squirrels. One feeder, the GSP, is fantastically weather-proof; for others such as the Cardinal Barn, it depends on the direction of the rain; still others, such as platform feeders, rate a zero in this category. Baldwin's Sheltered Birdfeeder takes advantage of the wind to protect the seed inside. Some feeders, such as the Droll Yankee, have sophisticated drainage systems to help keep the seed dry. But the type of feeder alone doesn't determine how resistant to weather it may be. Where you locate your feeder (is it sheltered by a fence or tree, or out in the open on a pole?) and how you baffle it also plays a role in the ability of the feeder to withstand Mother Nature. If your feeder spills too much seed or gets too wet after a storm you may need to replace that feeder—or you may simply need to move it.

Care of Your Feeders and Your Birds
Squirrels alone don't contribute to the demise of feeders. Although their daily climbing, clawing, and biting regimen can cloud, scar, and weaken feeders, fluctuating temperatures, hail, bird droppings, falling berries, small children, and mildew all take a toll on birdfeeders. Fortunately many birdfeeders are inexpensive enough to replace from time to time, but with a minimum of cleaning a feeder will last years. It's important to clean your feeder periodically for another reason: moisture and seed make mold which may kill birds. Wash your feeder with hot water and soap once every couple of months. That's all. Use only nonabrasive soaps, disinfectants, and cleaning pads because plastic feeders easily scratch, and the more scratches the less visibility. Dry the feeder thoroughly, refill it, and enjoy. If the seed inside becomes damp after a storm, discard that seed, dry (or clean) the feeder, and refill. I know it goes against the grain to throw away seed, but it's much better to waste some birdseed than to see you favorite titmice in legs-up position. Remember, the birds trust you.

Many feeders collect moisture. Bowl-shaped feeders, some window feeders, and multi-tube feeders can gather considerable moisture. In addition, birds hop around the inside of some feeders and defecate on the seed, which can turn healthy seed into deadly seed overnight. Inspect your feeders regularly for moisture and droppings. Heidi Hughes, proprietor of the Wild Bird Company in Rockville, Maryland, says, "when it rains, discarded sunflower seed shells act as a wick, sopping up water and mold." Hughes says the flatter the feeder the better. Check your feeder regularly for moisture content.

There's a debate over whether a feeder should spill seed onto the ground. When seed spills—or when birds flick undesirable seed—ground-feeding birds such as mourning doves and cardinals are attracted. However, **seed on the ground quickly becomes moldy, especially after a rain. In addition, seed below a feeder gets contaminated with bird droppings. Moldy seed and seed covered with droppings are vectors for disease, including salmonella and deadly avian pox. If you notice any bird looking ill especially around the eye or beak, switch feeders, remove spilled seed from the ground every day, and consider placing a seed catcher below the feeder.** Always keep in mind that bird droppings and moisture poison seed.

You can reduce the amount of seed that spills to the ground by avoiding seed mixes. When a bird encounters a seed it doesn't like, the bird flicks that seed to the ground. Feeders with a single seed inside have much lower spillage. The safest arrangement is to have several feeders, each with its own seed.

It's very hard to find a feeder that doesn't spill any seed to the ground. And it's very hard to curtail the desire for spilled seed because it attracts such wonderful birds. What to do? If you're worried about spillage, buy a feeder that has little spillage, such as Looker Products' SPF. In addition, you can buy feeding platforms with drainage.

Feeders can pose another danger to birds. Birds, especially small ones like chickadees, can enter feeders with holes of an inch or more, as well as get inside "barn"-like feeders. And birds may try to get inside these feeders when they can't reach the seed by just sticking their head in the opening. Once inside they can't escape. A feeder with a 1 inch or larger hole that is low on seed can be a death-trap for birds. You must keep these feeders full or have an second feeder to attract birds because a bird may crawl inside and get stuck.

I'd like to mention a couple of miscellaneous—but crucial—points about birdfeeders. First, always, always, always, wash you hands with hot water and soap after handling your feeder or birdseed. **Never** handle your feeder when you have an unbandaged cut or other open wound on your hand. This is especially true for small children who are forever putting their fingers in their mouths: keep them away from the feeder. Birds are pretty, their songs sweet, and they are plenty of fun to watch, but they carry dangerous diseases. Their droppings are filled with bacteria that is harmful to birds and to you. If you'd like to know what you can catch from birds, here's the short list:

Hypersensitivity pneumonitis, an allergy, sometimes called pigeon breeder's disease.

Psittacosis, a lung infection that gives you many hours of a hacking cough, severe headache, chills, fever and loss of appetite.

Histoplasmosis, a fungal disease whose symptoms resemble tuberculosis.

Cryptococcosis, a fungus that causes meningitis.

Salmonellosis, a bacterial infection that produces food poisoning.

Try not to purchase too much seed in advance, because it decays with age, especially hulled and cracked seeds. As a general rule the warmer and more humid it is the shorter the lifetime of the birdseed. Seed won't last longer than one season. Unless. Unless you refrigerate or freeze it, which may not be the most energy efficient scheme, but does have several benefits. Besides preserving your seed, freezing kills bugs. Stephanie Faul, a Washington, D.C. birder, passed this tidbit along to me. Whenever she bought seed in bulk, lots of flying critters appeared along with the seed, and Stephanie, who lives in an apartment, wasn't pleased with releasing moths inside, even if her cats adored the situation. Now Stephanie puts the bags of feed in her freezer for a few days and voila—no bugs.

A few pages ago I mentioned that a feeder's location plays a role in how squirrel-resistant it is, and how easily you can fill the feeder. But location matters to what's underneath the feeder as well. Wherever you place your feeder you are going to accumulate lots of bird droppings. Still worse, the shells from sunflower seeds and spillage of hulled sunflowers will kill the lawn beneath. So wherever you put your feeder, consider the ground underneath a dead zone.

Feeders should be put close enough to your house so you can see them, but not too close so that you scare the birds. By the same token, don't put your feeder near the picnic table because every time you eat at the table the birds are going to fly away.

THE MANDARIN

Type: Hanging feeder
Dimensions: 17" × 17"
Seed capacity: Over 5 quarts
Attracts: Just about everything except nuthatches. Downy woodpeckers will occasionally feed at the Mandarin; cardinals, juncos, and mourning doves enjoy the seed that spills to the ground. You'll even see blackbirds at this feeder. Starlings love the Mandarin.

The Mandarin is among the most uniquely-shaped feeders. A fat cylindrical tub with four holes and perches in it is covered by something that looks like an upside-down funnel with a skirt. Both the funnel and skirt are steep. The entire feeder is constructed out of rigid, transparent plastic. The skirt angles down over the perches, providing a roof.

The Mandarin is supported by a chain that extends into the center of the feeder. You refill the Mandarin by lifting the funnel-skirt, raising this lid, and pouring the seed in. Unlike most feeders, the Mandarin has a huge opening—over 6 inches in diameter—through which you can pour seed; there's very little spillage during this frequently wasteful process. You have to hold the top while filling the feeder (it doesn't come off) but that doesn't present any problem.

Birds are visible from three sides. Like all four-sided feeders, you can block off the opening that doesn't face your window. The birds won't mind.

This feeder gets covered with bird droppings fairly quickly. Fortunately, it can be cleaned in minutes. The Mandarin is as close to 100% percent squirrel-proof as you can buy. It and the GSP feeder stand in a class of their own. I've watched for hours as squirrels attempt to leap to the perches, which offer little landing room—they fail each time. I've been amused by squirrels' attempts to reach over the top and either feed upside down or catch the perch from above—they either give up or fall to the ground. They keep falling and trying again. I've even seen adventurous squirrels try to lift the top of the feeder, which is too heavy and cumbersome. Unlike lighter feeders, they can't knock and spill seed out.

Sarah Abrams of Arlington, Virginia has this to say about her Mandarin feeder:

> I have hung it on a straight metal arm. The arm is attached to my wooden back porch, which stands several feet above the ground. This means the feeder's ports hang about four and a half feet above the ground and about 30" out from the porch railing. I filled it with black oil sunflower seeds.
>
> The squirrels climb out on the arm but seem uneasy when they reach the far end of the arm and it no doubt begins to bend under them. One or two of the more adventurous squirrels have tried hanging upside down from the chain (which is 8-10" long,) but apparently decided they cannot get down the steeply-sloped feeder roof. None of them has tried jumping to the perches. In the end, all give up and scavenge for whole seeds among the dropped hulls on the ground.

Still, the Mandarin isn't perfectly squirrel-proof. Heidi Hughes reported that one of her customers brought back a Mandarin "that looked like someone had taken a sledgehammer to it. The squirrel ate through the top." Hughes surmises that apparently in the Midwest, where the Mandarin is manufactured, "squirrels aren't as aggressive as they are in the East." Fortunately, the manufacturer is working on a modified top with an additive that squirrels won't be able to gnaw through.

The Mandarin has three flaws. First, when the feeder starts to run out of seed it becomes increasingly difficult for birds to get at that seed; chickadees may go after that last seed by crawling inside. Once inside they can become trapped and die, "which is a horrible sight," reported Heidi Hughes. **Never** let the Mandarin get too low on seed (or make sure that you have another feeder for birds.) Second, finches are crazy about it. Third, seed can spill from the feeder at high rates. When birds eat unevenly from one side, the feeder becomes unbalanced and high energy birds such as starlings and finches can knock seed to the ground. This seed can quickly become wet and moldy and become a source of disease for birds.

Mandarin	Poor					Great
Squirrel-proofness						X
Ease of refilling						X
Visibility of birds					X	
Seed capacity						X
Attractiveness				X		
Versatility of location				X		
Overall						X

GSP FEEDER

Type: Hanging feeder
Dimensions: 13″ in diameter
Seed capacity: Over 1½ gallons of seed
Attracts: Small birds such as finches, titmice, wrens, and downy woodpeckers. Peanuts will not work in the GSP feeder so peanut-loving birds won't be attracted to this feeder. Suet can be hung inside.

No other feeder has received as much attention as Dr. Stephen Clarke's GSP feeder. And deservedly so: the GSP design and abilities are innovative and a step beyond any other feeder on the market. It is the only feeder that birds fly up and into to eat. Through its shape, the GSP feeder provides complete protection from predators for birds as they eat; the GSP is also completely weatherproof. If you live in an area with a lot of rain or snow, the GSP could be the best feeder for you.

The GSP feeder is attractive, too. Its smooth curves are more reminiscent of a post-modern sculpture than a birdfeeder. It has an almost aerodynamic design. A muted aluminum cover, also curved, rests on top of the GSP and hides the opening through which seed is added. Instead of a chain, which most feeders use to hang, the GSP is supported by an aluminum pole. This simple addition gives the feeder a sense of durability and class; it also keeps the feeder from swaying in the wind.

The closest common geometry that the GSP feeder resembles is a dome. Birds fly into the expansive cavity and perch themselves on one of the two ledges through which seed is dispensed. There's room for about eight birds to eat at the same time—assuming they get along.

In his patent application, Dr. George Clarke described the GSP feeder this way:

> A birdfeeder comprising a body extending along a vertical axis, the body having an outer shell, a wall inside the shell, the shell and the wall defining a reservoir, the shell and the wall further defining a restricted chute, and a feed tray inside the shell, the chute communicating between the reservoir and the tray to provide gravity feed of seed, and a fly-in access opening in the shell, the access opening communicating between the exterior of the shell and the tray and being large enough to allow birds to fly into the shell, the extent of the shell between the opening and the upper end of the body being large enough to prevent squirrels resting on the end from reaching into the opening.

The original GSP feeder contained a minor design flaw which a handful of squirrels could take advantage of. These ultra-smart squirrels lifted the aluminum top with one paw, braced themselves with another, and stuck their heads into the rectangular opening used for refilling the GSP. As uncomfortable as it was, these few squirrels were able to feast on the GSP. Current models of the GSP feeder contain a latch that fits around the aluminum pole and over the top. Because of this latch (sometimes called the Rodney lock) you need two hands to lift the top—something squirrels don't have—yet.

I was one of those who encountered a super-smart squirrel. After I watched a squirrel lift the lid I wrote to Clarke Products:

March 4, 1987

Dear Clarke Products Company:
I am enjoying your feeder. Of all the bird feeders I've used—
about six different kinds—it took squirrels the longest to get into
yours.

Here's how Rodney the squirrel (not his real name) did it. My
GSP feeder is attached to the side of my apartment building with
a two-foot long pole, angled up at 45°. Rodney quickly determined that he couldn't enter the feeder from the bottom. However, by supporting himself with his back claws from the brick
building and hanging upside down, Rodney managed to raise the
aluminum top high enough so that he could stick his head inside
the space used to refill the feeder.

I've had the feeder for nine days. He got in yesterday.

Rodney doesn't mind eating while upside down.

Actually, it's taken Rodney the squirrel less time to figure out
how to get inside than some of the birds that were customers of
my previous feeder.

Perhaps I'm not being fair. After all, I labored hard devising
all sorts of apparatuses and Rube Goldberg concoctions around
my former feeders to keep Rodney and his friends out. I expect
that he became an exceptionally clever squirrel during those trying
months.

So, let me suggest a minor modification on the GSP feeder. A
latch (instead of the package sealing tape I'm now using) would
be helpful in securing the aluminum top to the rest of the feeder.

Sincerely,
Bill Adler

Dr. Clarke wrote back:

March 9, 1987

Rodney c/o Bill Adler
2800 Devonshire Pl., N.W.
Washington, D.C. 20008
Dear Rodney:
I have good new and bad news. First, the good news. You have
succeeded in 9 days of doing something that in four years of
testing the GSP in the Northeast, no other squirrel did. With five

thousand feeders sold, you have two other cousins, one in Simsbury, Ct. and one in Grosse Point, Mich. who also learned the trick.

Now for the bad news. Your master will install the enclosed "Rodney Lock"—it gets your name because the other cousins of yours are nameless—and I fear this will curtail your dining.

You see, it sits on top of the aluminum cover and it takes two hands to open the feeder. One slides the Rodney Lock up to the top of the hanger. It will stay there. Then the top is lifted and the feeder is filled. The Rodney Lock then drops back into position.

Sorry, Rodney.
Very truly yours,
Stephen G. Clarke, Pres.

Before the GSP, no feeder designer took advantage of the simple fact that birds fly and squirrels don't.[1] Feeders have to be attached to something—usually a pole or a hanging chain—and squirrels merely have to scale that support to reach the feed. But the GSP's principle is that the feed should be placed in a part of the feeder that can only be accessed by creatures that fly. To get to the GSP's feed, an animal has to fly *up*; there's no way to climb into the seed compartment. Squirrels do get on top of the GSP, but because the feeder curves around like a beach ball, squirrels can't climb around to reach the opening on the bottom.

The inventor of the GSP, University of Connecticut Professor Stephen G. Clarke, said, "I say let's give the birds a chance." The GSP was exhibited at the 15th Annual Inventors Expo sponsored by the Patent and Trademark Office in 1987.

It's fun to watch squirrels try to get into the GSP. They can't, but never seen to learn that fact.

You refill the GSP by first lifting the bracket, the Rodney lock. They you lift the aluminum cover to expose a roughly 1" by 2"

[1]One birder, however, isn't so sure about this. I thank Walter Stolwein for letting me reproduce his original poem here:

The Pest
The squirrel is a furry bird
Or thinks he is, upon my word
It hogs the feeder's costly seeds
Ignoring feathered birdies' needs.

rectangular opening. You definitely need a seed dispenser to fill the GSP; otherwise filling it is straightforward. The seed spills into the cavities on both sides.

Sunflower seeds work best with the GSP; peanuts don't work at all.

And although it doesn't say so in the manual, there's enough room inside the GSP to hang a suet cake. Just attach the cake to a wire and wrap the wire around the inside bolt. Woodpeckers love this indoor dining.

The GSP's drawback is that sometimes it's hard to see the birds. After a short time, the GSP becomes dirty on both the inside and outside. There's no problem seeing birds flutter around outside, but once they decide to venture in to snack, they can be hard to see. In addition, if the GSP rotates (or a squirrel rotates it) so that one of the two seed cavities faces you, you won't be able to see birds inside at all.

GSP	Poor				Great
Squirrel-proofness					X
Ease of refilling					X
Visibility of birds	X				
Seed capacity				X	
Attractiveness				X	
Versatility of location			X		
Overall				X	

THE STEEL SQUIRREL-PROOF FEEDER (SPF)

Type: Fortress post feeder
Dimensions: Roof is 12½" × 12½", about 9" high
Seed capacity: 2 gallons

Attracts: Cardinals, titmice, starlings, wrens, chickadees, finches, blue jays, and mockingbirds; mourning doves are attracted to the spilled seed.

The SPF was created by Looker Products in Milford, Illinois. Inventors Olin and Caroline Looker wanted to create a feeder that was squirrel-proof and didn't waste any seed. The result was the Steel Squirrel-Proof Feeder, or SPF.

The SPF is a clever feeder, relying on the principle that squirrels weigh more than birds. When a squirrel lands on the platform, his weight causes a shield to close in front of the seed. When the squirrel leaves the platform, the aluminizedsteel shield opens again. Two steel springs in the back of the feeder can be adjusted to vary the weight that causes the shield to shut, so that heavy birds can be prevented from entering. The SPF looks a little like a fortress, and as far as squirrels are concerned, it is. They can't lift the shield and they can't bite through the metal.

The SPF is covered with a weather resistant, light green enamel paint. The platform is made of cedar. Unlike plastic feeders that become scratched and cloudy over the years, or wooden feeders that get gnawed by squirrels or become water damaged, the SPF should last practically forever.

The SPF's large seed capacity means that a week can go by without your having to refill the feeder. The SPF mounts on a pole or post, and by placing a baffle beneath it you can increase its anti-squirrel capabilities.

The SPF is easily refilled by lifting a latch that secures the top in place, and then lifting the hinged top. The inside walls of the SPF tilt downward, drawing the seed into the bin. Because all the seed reaches the opening in front of the platform, there won't be any leftover seed that can become moldy. Almost every kind of seed works with the SPF, including sunflower seed and shelled peanuts. By varying the seed, you can attract or discourage particular birds.

In fact, you may want to fill the feeder with exclusively black oil sunflower seeds, to discourage starlings, who don't care for sunflower seeds. If this feeder has a flaw it's that starlings can make a mess of the seed and spill a good amount (something they can do to most feeders). If you want to discourage birds from flicking seed to the ground, fill the SPF with one type of seed at a time.

The SPF wins the award in the "Ecologically Sound" category. Because seed stays completely dry and because when filled with a single seed type there's little spillage, there's little chance that seed will become moldy. There's also no opportunity for small birds to get inside and become trapped. For people who care about the well-being of their birds, the SPF is an excellent choice.

Up to six small birds or three larger ones can feed at a time. Because the feeder doesn't move, you will always see the birds as they eat.

SPF	Poor				Great
Squirrel-proofness					X
Ease of refilling					X
Visibility of birds				X	
Seed capacity					X
Attractiveness		X			
Versatility of location		X			
Overall					X

THE CARDINAL BARN AND OTHER WOODEN FEEDERS

Type: Wooden hanging feeder, usually constructed out of cedar or redwood (various designs all shaped like a chalet, with two glass or plastic sides, a redwood roof, base, and sides. These wooden feeders can be hung or mounted.)
Dimensions: Varies from roughly 12″ × 10″ × 9″ to 20″ × 15″ × 12″
Seed capacity: 3 to 10 pounds.
Attracts: Cardinals, finches, chickadees, titmice, blackbirds, nuthatches, wrens, small woodpeckers, pine siskins, and starlings. Considerable spillage also attracts mourning doves and juncos.

Wooden feeders are great because they are easy to fill, have large seed capacities, and when they offer good bird watching, the watching is very good. But because they move while hanging, there are times when birds are completely obscured. These feeders are not so terrific in the squirrel-proof department.

But they are made of wood: wood is pleasant and natural; it always looks better than plastic (at least in the beginning). Birds like it more and so do people. But there's a downside to wood: bird droppings show up more prominently. After a while you may pray for rain.

Wooden feeders are usually filled by lifting the roof and pouring the seed in. The seed spills out along troughs on the two long sides. It's easy for just about any bird to feast at the cardinal barn. Seed spillage brings in plenty of ground-feeding birds, but it can also bring deadly mold and avian pox.

When the cardinal barn becomes low on seed, birds may try to go after that last seed or two by pushing up the plastic sides and slipping inside, where they become imprisoned. As with other feeder that small birds can slip into, be careful when this feeder starts to run low on seed.

The cardinal barn and other wooden hanging feeders have another drawback: they are squirrel attractors. Squirrels throughout the neighborhood know when there's a new wooden feeder around. Perhaps they can smell the wood, or perhaps they're just attracted to it as they're attracted to trees. Whatever the reason, hanging the cardinal barn is like an invitation to a party—and you are providing the goodies. Once the squirrels arrive at the feeder, they can choose to dine upright, sideways or upside-down; the wood is easy to cling to. And if the squirrels don't like the angles you've allowed them to eat from, they'll simply gnaw through the feeder in a few minutes. Wood doesn't provide much resistance to squirrel teeth. In fact, eating seed from the cardinal barn is so easy that squirrels will probably eat your feeder anyway, just to prove they're able to.

You can baffle classic wooden feeders, but unless you put your baffles around perfectly, you will have squirrels as guests. All they need to do is connect one paw to the feeder and they are in.

Cardinal Barn	Poor				Great
Squirrel-proofness	x to	x			
Ease of refilling					x
Visibility of birds		x			
Seed capacity					x
Attractiveness			x	to	x
Versatility of location				x	
Overall		x			

THE HYLARIOUS

Type: Fortress post feeder
Dimensions: 9" × 12" × 17"
Seed capacity: 8 quarts of seed
Attracts: Cardinals, titmice, starlings, wrens, chickadees, finches, blue jays, and mockingbirds; mourning doves are attracted to the spilled seed.

The Hylarious is similar in design and function to the SPF. Squirrels are prevented from entering the feeder by a shield that closes over the opening to the seed whenever a squirrel steps on the platform. While the SPF is green, the Hylarious is red. Both hold the same amount of seed.

There are some other differences between the SPF and the Hylarious. The seed in the Hylarious sits on a horizontal shelf, so not all the seed will be consumed. The platform that birds eat from and squirrels activate is metal, not wood.

Hylarious	Poor				Great
Squirrel-proofness				X	
Ease of refilling				X	
Visibility of birds					X
Seed capacity					X
Attractiveness		X			
Versatility of location			X		
Overall				X	

THE FOILER

Type: Fortress post feeder
Dimensions: 9" X 11" X 14"
Seed capacity: 10 quarts
Attracts: Cardinals, titmice, starlings, wrens, chickadees, finches, blue jays, and mockingbirds; mourning doves are attracted to the spilled seed.

One thing you have to say about many birdfeeders: their names get right to the point. The Foiler, another SPF-like feeder, works by using a squirrel's weight against him. As soon as a squirrel steps on the perching platform, his weight causes the seed hopper shield to cut off access to the seed. Sorry, Mr. Squirrel, no snack today.

The Foiler has a larger seed capacity than either the SPF or the Hylarious. It must be mounted on a special post, however. Six holes stand between the platform and the inside seed bin; these holes are designed to prevent pigeons and other large birds from getting to the seed.

Foiler	Poor					Great
Squirrel-proofness						X
Ease of refilling						X
Visibility of birds					X	
Seed capacity						X
Attractiveness	X					
Versatility of location	X					
Overall					X	

ESTATE FEEDER

Type: Pole feeder
Dimensions: Not applicable
Seed Capacity: 2+ quarts
Attracts: Finches, cardinals, titmice, chickadees, starlings, mockingbirds.

The Estate feeder is among the newest feeders marketed by the Duncraft company. It combines simplicity, an adequate seed capacity, effective anti-squirrel capabilities, and good bird visibility.

The Estate feeder is basically a 2 quart bowl that holds about 5 pounds of bird seed, situated on a pole. The feeder is positioned between a 16" baffle on the bottom and a 12" baffle on top. As long as you don't place the Estate feeder near any trees it should be virtually squirrel-proof; the baffle is impenetrable. For added protection you can place the feeder on a squirrel-spooker pole or grease the pole with vaseline.

To fill the Estate feeder all you have to do is pour seed from a dispenser into the bowl. If you use black sunflower or other shelled seed, some hulls will accumulate in the feeder, which is fine if you don't want them scattered all over your lawn, not so good if you're adverse to emptying the feeder frequently.

The feeder is well protected from most rains, but a storm that moves rain horizontally will get the seed inside wet. The Estate feeder is impervious to snow, as long as the snowdrifts don't grow taller than the height of the pole.

Estate	Poor ————————————— Great				
Squirrel-proofness					X
Ease of refilling				X	
Visibility of birds					X
Seed capacity			X		
Attractiveness		X			
Versatility of location			X		
Overall				X	

SQUIRREL'S DILEMMA

Type: Hanging feeder
Dimensions: 5''' square × 19'' long.
Seed capacity: 4–8 pounds
Attracts: Most birds including titmice, wrens, lots of finches, chickadees and nuthatches. Cardinals and mourning doves will feed off the seed that falls to the ground.

The Squirrel's Dilemma is a long, rectangular feeder constructed of clear styrene plastic and surrounded with reinforced fox wire. Concave openings in the plastic dispense the seed. It reminds one of a medieval fortress, its forbidding shape silently shouting a warning to potential intruders: do not venture near. Access to the feed is gained by sticking a beak in between the small spaces in the wire. The wire also provides a perch for little feathered friends.

The Squirrel's Dilemma lets you watch birds from three sides. If you want, you can cover the openings on the fourth side to force birds to eat only from the places where you can view them. The feeder itself won't win awards for design excellence; it's rather bland-looking. However, its long shape and wire exterior keep the feeder miraculously free of droppings.

The Squirrel's Dilemma can be hung from a post or tree limb.

Refilling the Squirrel's Dilemma isn't difficult, but you do have to remove the entire feeder to replenish it. Refilling is a simple matter of opening the metal top and pouring the seed in.

As for its squirrel-resistance, if you *enjoy* feeding squirrels, the Squirrel's Dilemma is for you. When hung alone, without any baffles or other obstructions, it takes squirrels about ninety seconds to figure out how dine at the Squirrel's Dilemma. Although it's true that squirrels "cannot chew on the feeder or get their head through the wire," as one bird supply catalog insists, they can get their mouths through, and that's all squirrels care about. No squirrel was ever scolded by its parents because it brought its face to the food instead of the other way around. And I've never seen a squirrel forsake a sunflower seed-at-a-time meal, especially when they can gobble at about twenty seeds a minute. Squirrels can also stick a paw inside and slide the seed into their ready mouths. The fox-wire grid lets squirrels arrange themselves on the outside of the feeder in the position that's most comfortable to them. What a deal! While squirrels may have a hard time draining the Squirrel's Dilemma because they can't gorge themselves, they will hang around this reliable food source.

The Squirrel's Dilemma is a tough feeder to baffle because all a squirrel has to do is get one paw anywhere along any of the feeder's 19-inch sides to gain access. So even with a baffle, an agile squirrel can maneuver itself so it reaches some part of the feeder.

Despite the Squirrel Dilemma's attractiveness to squirrels, it is a fun feeder. Squirrels really can't empty it (at least not right away) and it does let you feed a variety of birds with a minimum of inconvenience. Some birds will even eat from the feeder on one side, while a squirrel is invisibly snacking on the other. Feeders with large seed capacities and good visibility are always welcome.

Duncraft's squirrel-proof Estate Feeder attracts a variety of birds. In this photo two goldfinches are dining. Photo courtesy Duncraft, Penacook, N.H.

This squirrel solved the Squirrel's Dilemma by eating upside down.

Squirrel's Dilemma	Poor				Great
Squirrel-proofness	X				
Ease of refilling			X		
Visibility of birds				X	
Seed capacity				X	
Attractiveness		X			
Versatility of location			X		
Overall		X			

THE CLING-A-WING

Type: Hanging feeder
Dimensions: 6″ in diameter
Seed capacity: 1 quart
Attracts: When filled with nuts this feeder will attract blue jays and red-bellied woodpeckers. Some people use this feeder exclusively as their nut feeder. Also attracts finches, titmice, nuthatches, evening grosbeaks, and wrens.

The Cling-a-Wing is a cute feeder. It's a plastic globe with four openings where birds can perch and eat. Smaller birds such as titmice, chickadees, and of course, finches, adore the Cling-a-Wing, but woodpeckers also eat from it when there's nothing else around. The globe prevents the seed inside from getting wet.

You refill the Cling-a-Wing by lifting the plastic stopper and pouring seed inside. You can use your hands to fill this feeder, but a seed dispenser works much better. The Cling-a-Wing can hold a variety of seed including sunflower seed, bread crumbs, and peanuts. In addition, a suet cake holder can be attached to the bottom of the Cling-a-Wing with bell wire wrapped around the bottom nut.

Although you can only see birds eating from one side, it's small enough so that you're bound to see birds flying around looking for a place to land. The Cling-a-Wing also rotates so that birds eating on the feeder's hidden side may come into view as they eat.

The Cling-a-Wing is only partially squirrel-proof. If hung on a window bracket, squirrels can usually reach out from the wall and pull the feeder toward them. They can also attack from above by holding on to the ring on top of the feeder with their claws and munching upside down. If squirrels are having a difficult time eating the birdseed, they will eat the feeder. The Cling-a-Wing is among the most-often-chewed birdfeeders around. They gnaw at the openings to make them bigger and they'll gnaw at the plastic belt around the feeder's equator. As they attack, squirrels will manage to spill a considerable amount of seed, which helps ground-feeding birds, but also encourages squirrels as well.

A large baffle placed close to the globe will keep squirrels from reaching the seed. The baffle will also make it more difficult to fill the Cling-a-Wing, but that's a common trade-off.

Cling-a-wing	Poor —————————— Great				
Squirrel-proofness		X			
Ease of refilling	X				
Visibility of birds				X	
Seed capacity		X			
Attractiveness			X		
Versatility of location		X			
Overall		X			

THE SPINNING SATELLITE

Type: Hanging feeder
Dimensions: 6″ diameter
Seed capacity: About 1 pound.

Attracts: Titmice, chickadees, finches, downy woodpeckers. The feeder cannot be filled with whole nuts, but can support peanut hearts.

It is perhaps the cutest bird feeder. The Spinning Satellite looks like a modern version of the spaceship on the old TV program, "My Favorite Martian." As it hangs it spins in the wind or after a bird takes off from it. The feeder's diminutive size and symmetrical shape make it a pleasing feeder to look at. Chickadees think so. So do titmice, finches, and other small birds.

Unfortunately, squirrels think it's cute as well.

Cute is one attribute you shouldn't be looking for in a birdfeeder. Attractive, maybe; but definitely not cute.

Here's how this cute birdfeeder works. The Spinning Satellite is shaped like a nearly perfect globe. There's a circular opening underneath the satellite's equator, which has a little lip that serves as a perch. And the equator is a plastic protrusion that encircles the entire globe like Saturn's rings. The purpose of this protrusion is to keep squirrels from getting into the feeding hole. Amazingly, it accomplishes that objective—for about six seconds.

Squirrels may, if they feel like it, reach over and feed from the Spinning Satellite from the top. From this position, feeding is more like feasting.

If you cover the Spinning Satellite with a baffle, which immediately destroys the Satellite's cute looks, squirrels can't feast from above.

So they latch on to the ring upside down and eat that way. From this position, they can empty the feeder quickly.

There's another option available to squirrels as well, one that is bound to please ground-feeding birds. It takes a little ingenuity or a dash of luck to figure out how to get the Spinning Satellite off its chain and on the ground. From there squirrels bat it around like a soccer ball. Another point about the Spinning Satellite: it holds a tiny amount of seed. And although only one bird at a time can eat from it, you'll find yourself filling and filling and filling the Spinning Satellite—probably every other afternoon.

And still another point about this feeder: despite its little size, filling it is a pain. After you remove the cap, you put in the seed. Unfortunately, most seed dispensers won't fit the Spinning Satellite. As you try to fill it with your hands, you end up planting sunflower seeds.

Which brings me to yet another point about the Spinning Satellite. It only holds sunflower seeds. Peanuts clog the feeder, and other seeds don't flow easily through it. Because the opening angles upward, there's very little seed spillage.

In rare cases chickadees can climb inside the Spinning Satellite and become trapped.

So are there any virtues to the Spinning Satellite? Yes. It's a good way to coax squirrels away from your regular feeders. And *it is* good looking. If you already have a feeder or two set up, then go ahead and buy the Spinning Satellite. It's a fun feeder to watch.

Spinning Satellite	Poor —————————————— Great				
Squirrel-proofness	X				
Ease of refilling	X				
Visibility of birds				X	
Seed capacity	X				
Attractiveness				X	
Versatility of location			X		
Overall	X				

THE WINDOW CHALET

Type: Window feeder
Dimensions: 9″ × 6″ × 4″
Seed Capacity: 1 quart
Attracts: Finches (lots), titmice, chickadees, wrens, downy woodpeckers, and blue jays (if you fill it with peanuts). Doves and cardinals will hang around for spilled seed.

The window chalet is a good-looking, chalet-style bird feeder. It attaches to your window with two suction cups, and holds a quart of seed, enough for one to three days depending on how many house finches you have. In addition to being attractive, the window chalet offers an excellent view of birds. You can stealthfully get within a foot of the feeder without scaring the birds away. It's an easy feeder to fill: either reach outside and fill by tilting a seed dispenser into it, or lift the feeder off the suction cups and fill it indoors. The feeder is simple to use, but can be difficult to install. When putting it on your window for the first time you'll find that the window chalet either ends up crooked or the suction cups keep falling to the ground. Which can be a big deal if you live in an apartment building, as I did. To attach the feeder correctly you must follow the instructions carefully, because gravity has a way of defeating suction cups over time. Installed properly, the window chalet should stay up for about a year or until there's a hurricane. Or until a squirrel finds it.

The window chalet is not squirrel-proof. In order for the window chalet to be squirrel-proof one of the following criteria must be met. A) It must be high enough from any surface so that squirrels can't jump in *and* it must be positioned so that squirrels can't jump on top and crawl inside, or B) there must not be any squirrels around. Clearly the last possibility is no possibility.

There are two ways a squirrel can attack the window feeder: by jumping or climbing in, or by leaping on top and crawling over the top. Once he's inside, Mr. Squirrel can eat away. When a squirrel leaps on or into the window chalet it stresses the suction cups, playing directly into gravity's hands. A handful of such leaps and the window feeder is a goner. And if there's brick below, hope that you're handy with superglue. If you live in a squirrel-infested area, then you may spend a lot of time running outside and looking for those semi-transparent suction cups on your hands and knees (just tell your neighbors it's your contact lens). On the other hand, having the feeder fall is better than coming home and finding a squirrel inside, wantonly feasting.

But if your feeder can be placed so that squirrels are unable to approach it, the window chalet is a gem. You may have to experiment to find out the perfect position to put it in.

The window chalet—and other window feeders—will stay on your window longer if you attach the suction cups with superglue. With superglue it will be able to resist a squirrel's weight.

Window Chalet	Poor				Great
Squirrel-proofness	x*				
Ease of refilling				x	
Visibility of birds					x
Seed capacity		x			
Attractiveness				x	
Versatility of location	x				
Overall		depends on location			

*unless in the middle of a large window

THE DOME FEEDER

Type: Hanging feeder
Dimensions: 7″ × 12″ diameter
Seed Capacity: About 1 quart
Attracts: Titmice, finches, blackbirds, chickadees, and blue jays, if you fill it with nuts and keep the opening large enough. Spillage attracts juncos, mourning doves, mockingbirds, and cardinals.

The dome feeder is a clever hanging feeder. A clear plastic tray that captures seed and shell and gives birds a place to perch is attached to a hexagonal hopper. The feeder is attached to a dome by a metal chain which can be raised or lowered depending on how squirrel-proof you want the feeder to be, and whether you want to prevent large birds from getting to the seed. The feeder and tray can be raised so that it is almost entirely inside the dome, which gives pretty good protection.

You get a fairly good view of birds, except of course when they're on the opposite side of the feeder. It can be filled with a variety of seeds including hulled sunflower, millet, and shelled peanuts.

The Spinning Satellite.

A house finch approaches the Dome Feeder.

You refill the dome feeder by lifting the chain that connects the feeder to the baffle and pouring seed in. You cannot fill the feeder while it is attached to the baffle.

You would think by looking at this feeder that it would be completely squirrel-proof when retracted within the dome. And it is. For awhile. After a couple of days some squirrel will figure out the way to thwart the dome feeder. Beating the dome feeder requires not so much smarts as it does athletic ability, so usually the strongest squirrel wins. A squirrel (because there usually isn't more than one around who can do it) defeats the dome feeder by hanging onto the ring on top of the dome with his hind legs, stretching over the baffle, leaning underneath the baffle, grabbing onto the tray, and pulling it towards him. When he leans, seed spills out the other side and less dominant squirrels also feast. Each successive time it's easier for the squirrel to gain access to the feeder. Because the dome feeder has such a small seed capacity, a squirrel can empty it in a hurry.

Dome Feeder	Poor ——————————————— Great				
Squirrel-proofness		x			
Ease of refilling				x	
Visibility of birds				x	
Seed capacity		x			
Attractiveness		x			
Versatility of location			x		
Overall			x		

THE CARDINAL CLASSIC

Type: Window feeder
Dimensions: 12″ × 5½″
Seed capacity: 1 quart

Attracts: Titmice, cardinals, finches (more than you've ever seen), chickadees, and sometimes nuthatches and mockingbirds. If you fill it with nuts you'll reduce your finch population and increase the number of chickadees, titmice, and blue jays who frequent this feeder.

The Cardinal Classic, a clear plastic feeder, is similar to the window chalet in application. The only differences between the Cardinal Classic and the window chalet is that three suction cups hold this feeder in place, rather than two, and it has a flat roof instead of an angled roof. The three suction cups are a little more difficult to attach, but they hold the feeder more securely in place. The Classic's flat roof makes it slightly easier for squirrels to enter than the window chalet. Some people prefer like this feeder's simple design over the window chalet's Swiss cottage style.

Cardinal Classic	Poor			Great
Squirrel-proofness	X			
Ease of refilling			X	
Visibility of birds			X	
Seed capacity	X			
Attractiveness	X			
Versatility of location		X		
Overall		X		

THE SONGBIRD TABLE FEEDER

Type: Open platform feeder
Dimensions: 21" × 18"
Seed capacity: Several quarts
Attracts: Everything.

The songbird table feeder can be a great feeder. The seed is visible to all birds. It attracts both ground-feeding birds, including cardinals and mourning doves, and birds that enjoy feeding up high, such as chickadees and titmice. You'll also see blue jays, woodpeckers, and just about everything else that flies.

The songbird table feeder can be mounted on a deck, fence post, or on top of a pole. It's simple to fill—just pour seed into it. It comes with a "moisture draining removable screen bottom" because this feeder *will* get wet. To clean the feeder simply remove the tray.

There are several drawbacks to the table feeder. A strong wind may knock seed out of the tray. When it rains the seed is going to get wet. Birds aren't crazy about wet seed; as seed dries it rots, so after a rain you should dump the seed and replace it. The feeder will become filled with bird droppings.

Most dangerously, the songbird table feeder can be squirrel heaven. Mounted on a deck or a fence, the feeder is an open invitation to squirrels. In fact some people use the table feeder to draw squirrels away from their other feeders. If you put the table feeder on a pole, make sure it's exceptionally well baffled.

Songbird Table	Poor ——————————— Great				
Squirrel-proofness	X				
Ease of refilling					X
Visibility of birds					X
Seed capacity				X	
Attractiveness		X			
Versatility of location		X			
Overall*					

*An overall rating is not possible given the peculiar nature of this feeder. Depending on how you intend to use it, it can either be terrific or you will be fending off squirrels all the time.

SUET BASKETS

Type: Specialized hanging feeder
Dimensions: Less than 5″ × 5″ × 2″
Seed capacity: 1 or 2 suet cakes
Attracts: Starlings, downies, red-bellied, red-headed, and other woodpeckers. Titmice also like suet, especially in winter, as do chickadees. Finches will gorge suet in winter, too, as will pretty much every bird.

Suet baskets aren't a particular brand of feeder, but because they are so popular, and so crucial to attracting particular kinds of birds such as woodpeckers, it's useful to know how best to use them. There are a number of variations on the theme, but generally suet feeders are rectangular baskets you place one or two suet cakes in. The feeders are open and birds can feed from any side.

Suet is beef fat. You can make it yourself, buy it from a butcher shop, or purchase commercially prepared suet. Most people prefer the latter course because commercially prepared suet cakes, though more expensive, are less messy. In addition, commercial suet lasts longer that home brews, which quickly rot in warm weather. There are several different "flavors" of commercial suet cakes—plain, suet filled with sunflower seed and millet, and peanut-filled suet. Suet is a high-energy food that provides many essential nutrients that birds would otherwise get from insects.

Most birders buy suet to attract woodpeckers all year round (downy, hairy, and red-bellied woodpeckers prefer suet to most other birdfeeder food,) and to offer a "well balanced" meal to other birds. The problem with suet is that it is a favorite meal for squirrels, who will eat it all year long. (Flying squirrels and raccoons also love suet, if you're wondering why your suet disappears overnight.) To compound this dilemma, woodpeckers prefer to eat suet near the tree trunk, which makes it easy for squirrels to reach the suet; dangling suet at the end of a branch won't attract woodpeckers. Baffles are worthless when used close to the tree trunk.

What to do? There are several solutions. First, create a squirrel diverter, a platform of sunflower seeds away from your feeder. Squirrels go for what's easiest. Second, place a metal skirt around the tree to keep squirrels from climbing it, assuming that's the only tree in the vicinity. Third, place the suet near the tree for a while. As woodpeckers become accustomed to your yard and as they begin to enjoy their free lunch, gradually move the suet further out on the branch. Now's the time for that baffle, which should cover the suet enough to keep squirrels from leaning over it, but not be too constricting for the larger woodpeckers. As you move the suet away from the tree, those woodpeckers will follow it.

Suet can solve a major problems many homeowners have: woodpeckers who drill holes in their house. Woodpeckers damage houses because they're looking for insects in the wood. With suet you'll tempt them away from your recently refurbished siding.

EXCLUSIVELY THISTLE FEEDERS

Type: Tubular feeder
Dimensions: Varies, the most common is 16″ long and about 2½″ wide.
Seed capacity: Approx. 2 quarts
Attracts: Finches, pine siskins, and red polls. To prevent house and purple finches from eating the thistle and to encourage only goldfinches, cut the perches to about 1/2″ long. House and purple finches will not be able to eat from these shortened perches.

Thistle feeders are specially designed to dispense only thistle seed. They have smaller openings than normal tube feeders. Thistle seed is also called niger, and is among the most expensive seed you can buy. But because you can modify the thistle feeder by shortening the perches to attract only goldfinches, it's a good feeder to have around.

It's best to buy the kind with wooden perches so that you can easily cut them. Metal perches are hard to cut. Another advantage of thistle feeders is that squirrels don't care for thistle, and will only eat it when they are one step before starving, or to bug you. Thistle feeders are also available as window feeders, which let you see goldfinches more closely.

If you modify your feeder to attract only goldfinches, the seed may not disappear so rapidly. Replace the thistle in the feeder at least once a month to prevent it from spoiling.

This feeder can be hung from a tree or mounted on a pole.

Thistle Feeders	Poor				Great
Squirrel-proofness					X
Ease of refilling		X			
Visibility of birds				X	
Seed capacity				X	
Attractiveness				X	
Versatility of location				X	
Overall				x*	

*Remember, this is a specialized feeder.

THISTLE/SUNFLOWER FEEDERS

Type: Tubular feeder
Dimensions: Varies, the most common is 16" long and about 2½" wide.
Seed capacity: Approx. 2 quarts
Attracts: Finches, titmice, chickadees, wrens; cardinals and mourning doves hang around to pick up the spilled seed (if you don't include a spill tray.)

What are called "thistle feeders" are usually feeders that can be filled with either thistle or sunflower or hulled seeds. Only those feeders with very small holes are pure thistle feeders. While the advantages of pure thistle feeders were highlighted in the previous pages, there is one implicit disadvantage: thistle only attracts a limited number of species. Sunflower, on the other hand, attracts most birds. Unfortunately it brings in squirrels like an insider stock tip brings in stock brokers.

Although thistle feeders hold two quarts of feed, as the seed level drops, fewer perches become available. If you want to make all perches feeding stations, you will have to refill this feeder fairly often.

Thistle feeders have a number of good points. They hold a relatively large amount of seed, are easy to hang, offer excellent viewing of birds, and can feed up to eight birds at a time. In addition, many come with spill trays that catch shells and falling seed. Birds have an easy time recognizing that they are filled with goodies and fly directly to them. Thistle feeders have a simple elegance about them, they're unpretentious, don't have any fancy gimmicks—all they do is feed birds. Thistle feeders feel right.

And they feel right for squirrels. Baffles are a must for thistle feeders. Because these feeders are so narrow, they can usually be hung far enough from the tree trunk to prevent squirrels from leaping to the feeder. If they do reach the feeder, squirrels can either hang upside down and eat, or stand on one of the perches—it's up to them.

If you mount your thistle feeder on a pole, be sure to baffle it below (and above if there are any trees in the vicinity.)

Like all feeders, thistle feeders should be cleaned on a regular basis.

Thistle/Sunflower	Poor ———————— Great			
Squirrel-proofness	x*			
Ease of refilling		x		
Visibility of birds				x
Seed capacity	x			
Attractiveness	x			
Versatility of location				x
Overall	x			

*Squirrel-proofness depends on how you baffle and hang this feeder; by itself it's open game for squirrels.

The Presto Galaxy Deluxe 3 Tube Bird Feeder

Type: Tubular hanging feeder
Dimensions: Three connected tubes, each 1¾" × 24"

Seed capacity: Approximately 6 quarts

Attracts: Titmice, chickadees, purple, house and goldfinches, wrens, cardinals, and mourning doves.

When you bought this feeder, you've bought a mouthful—for the birds. The Presto Galaxy Deluxe 3 Tube Bird Feeder is a tube feeder—actually three tube feeders connected together. It's similar in application to the regular thistle seed feeder; the 3 Tube can hold thistle, sunflower seed, hulled sunflower seed, millet, or cracked corn. The major differences between the two feeders are 1) the 3 Tube's size—it can accommodate up to 24 birds at a time—and 2) it cannot be mounted on a pole. This is a hanging feeder only.

But it's a fun feeder. Even if you aren't crazy about the amount of seed finches eat, you have to be amused by the way they carry on, and the 3 Tube attracts flocks of finches. If you've never seen 24 birds feed at the same time, it's worth investing in the 3 Tube. It may not be your regular feeder, but since the main reason for feeding birds is fun you should have a fun feeder.

The 3 Tube is not particularly squirrel-resistant. The largest baffle only barely covers the top. There's room for 24 birds, which means there are 24 places for squirrels to eat from. All those perches make it an easy target, especially because the three tubes add up to a wide feeder.

You have to refill three separate tubes, and if birds eat unevenly from one of the outside tubes you'll need to refill it to prevent the feeder from tilting and the seed from spilling. As with all tube feeders, frequent refilling is mandatory if you want all perching stations to be open at all times.

But is the 3 Tube worthwhile buying? Sure—if your frustration and fun levels are high enough. The 3 Tube definitely is a second feeder, not a first.

The Deluxe 3 Tube Hanging Feeder also comes in a thistle seed version.

In the early 1900s, because of hunting and deforestation, there was some concern that gray squirrels could become extinct.

The Presto Galaxy Deluxe 3 Tube Bird Feeder may not be the most squirrel-resistant feeder on the market, but it is one of the most fun. The Presto Galaxy attracts more birds at one time than just about any other feeder. Photo courtesy Presto Galaxy, Inc.

Presto Galaxy	Poor				Great
Squirrel-proofness	X				
Ease of refilling		X			
Visibility of birds					X
Seed capacity					X
Attractiveness		X			
Versatility of location	X				
Overall			X		

THE SQUIRREL BAFFLE BIRD FEEDER

Type: Hanging feeder
Dimensions: 14″ baffle dome with a 7″ seed hopper
Seed capacity: 5 pounds
Attracts: Chickadees, titmice, finches, wrens.

The Squirrel Baffle Bird Feeder (SBBF) is one of those feeders that you can't wait to get home to try. The picture and description on the box are tempting: "When squirrel tries to get at the food, the TILT ACTION causes him to slide off," reads the box. Finally, justice.

The SBBF can be filled with a variety of seed, including whole and shelled nuts, cracked corn, and sunflower seed. Everything fits comfortably in a bowl-like container. The bowl hooks into a baffle.

Its large baffle sways in the wind, which discourages birds and may occasionally spill seed, but it does protect the feeder from squirrels. Large birds aren't crazy about the SBBF because they can't get under the baffle easily. But it is a chickadee paradise. Birds are completely sheltered as they eat.

Squirrels that land on top slip off the SBBF faster than they fall off any other feeder. They'll keep trying, but it takes an exceptionally agile squirrel to get the seed in the SBBF. I can't imagine that a squirrel would gain more energy eating the seed inside than it would expend trying to get inside.

Squirrel Baffle	Poor				Great
Squirrel-proofness					X
Ease of refilling			X		
Visibility of birds				X	
Seed capacity				X	
Attractiveness	X				
Versatility of location			X		
Overall				X	

The Squirrel Baffle Bird Feeder keeps seed dry and out of squirrels' mouths.

6

Over-the-Counter Anti-Squirrel Structures and Devices

There was a complaint about a squirrel jumping from a tree to the roof of the Trinity Church. It has been found that the squirrel is jumping from a County tree so this is not a problem or responsibility of the Borough.
Rocky Hill Gazette, Rocky Hill, NJ

There are plenty of birdfeeders on the market. Some of these have a modicum of anti-squirrel abilities. Others are grazing stations for famished rodents. But even the feeders with the highest anti-squirrel capabilities aren't always squirrel-proof. Buying a feeder labeled "squirrel-proof" usually leads to disappointment. Often a manufacturer claims a feeder is squirrel-proof—and then you get it home and within two days you have the suspicion that that particular feeder must have been tested on Alaska's north slope, where there are no squirrels. Strong, persistent squirrels can figure out a way to penetrate most so-called anti-squirrel feeders. Whether a squirrel will penetrate a feeder is not a matter of **if**, but of **when**. Friendly squirrels teach their comrades this skill.

Even a good squirrel-thwarting feeder frequently needs to be improved on. You may have to put it on a pole. Or add a baffle. Or extend the chain the feeder's hanging from. But squirrels can climb poles, crawl over baffles, and shimmy chains and cords. These traditional tools for barring squirrel attacks often fail. Instead, you have to use the one great advantage that humans have over rodents—imagination. Some bird supply companies have done the thinking for you, and offer excellent anti-squirrel devices. Some of these over-the-counter devices work famously. But it may be necessary in other circumstances to let your imagination roam in your basement, garage, kitchen, or local hardware store, to find the material to construct your own anti-squirrel apparatus.

Keep in mind that where you place your feeder is as important as what feeder you buy or how you reinforce it. The effectiveness of anti-squirrel measures depends greatly on where you put the feeder in the first place. Trees seem to be a popular location for feeders, but popularity doesn't translate into effectiveness. Trees are not your friends; they are on the squirrel's side. Squirrels climb trees, live in trees, jump from tree to tree, eat trees, hide in trees, mate in trees. When you put a feeder in a tree you are placing your feeder in jeopardy. Baffle it well and bind it securely to the tree, or the squirrels will figure out a way to get at the feeder or knock the feeder down. (See the previous chapter, Rating the Feeders, for more on where to place your feeder.) Begin to ignore the trees in your yard and you will have taken the first step toward creating a squirrel-proof structure.

A couple of safety tips are in order here. While it helps birds to feed them, not all bird-feeding practices are healthy. Moisture, for example, creates a medium for mold to grow on seed. So, as you make your feeder squirrel-proof:

1. Place your feeder where it isn't likely to become soaked in a rainstorm. Baffles help keep feeders dry.
2. Discard the seed, clean and dry the feeder whenever it becomes wet.
3. Be leery about spilled seed. Although spilled seed attracts cardinals, juncos, mourning doves and other ground-feeding birds, seed on the ground quickly becomes wet and moldy.

In addition, seed beneath a feeder gets covered with bird droppings, which are vectors for diseases that kill birds.

4. Look out for your own health, too: always wash your hands after handling a feeder.

This points are covered in more detail in Chapter 5, Rating the Feeders.

If you don't consider your squirrel problem serious enough to take the countermeasures described in this chapter, just wait. Once the squirrels get a taste for things in your yard, there's no stopping them, as one birder observed in a letter to the editor of the *Dick E. Bird News*:

> I started feeding a cute little red squirrel that was hanging around my Birdsnest Boarding House. I brought him a variety of nuts and treated him royally. Now I find he is beginning to eat my new deck.
>
> —Nuts up North

(The *Dick E. Bird News* is a monthly newspaper about birds, birdseed, squirrels, and related affairs. It combines facts and amusement. For subscription information, write to P.O. Box 377, Acme, MI 49610. It's a publication no birder should be without.)

PART I: PASSIVE MEASURES

Teflon Greasing poles with oil is one of the oldest ways of preventing squirrels from climbing into feeders. All you do is coat the pole with WD-40 or other greasy stuff that's been in your basement, or let a teenager rub against it. It's entertaining to watch the grease work as the squirrels slide off. For awhile. For some squirrels.

Until it rains.

Even if it doesn't rain, squirrels will persist at trying to climb up a greased pole, and eventually the slick grease will turn pebbly. When that happens they can simply climb over it.

Grease has other limitations, too. Phil Stone of Washington, D.C. said that his wife, Katharine, once greased a pole in winter. The grease kept the squirrels off until it froze one cold day, and the squirrels simply shimmied up the ice. And for anyone who doubted this story, there were claw marks in the ice.

Fortunately, technology has brought us a new weapon: teflon. In particular, spray teflon in a can. All you do is spray it on the pole, and watch the fun as the first squirrel tries to climb the pole, side of your house or apartment building, or wherever you've put the feeder. (Don't spray teflon or oil in the baffle or any other place where birds might alight.) The teflon causes the slipping squirrel to blame its parents for incomplete climbing lessons.

Teflon is a good, temporary measure. I emphasize temporary because although it lasts longer than oil, when left outside the teflon will eventually come off the pole. Use teflon when you want a way of buying time until you can think of more permanent measures.

Nixalite When you've reached the stage that you have to use Nixalite to keep squirrels away from your feeder, you have very serious squirrel problems. Nixalite is dangerous-looking material. It can be a potent, almost impenetrable barrier. Nixalite is the last line of defense before you have to employ active, threatening methods, like buying a big dog. Once you've used Nixalite you have surely declared war on squirrels. So before Nixalite, be warned: Once Nixalite appears, squirrels will know that they no longer have to play Mr. Nice Rodent.

Nixalite was developed in the late 1940s and has been marketed by Nixalite of America since 1950 as a method for controlling— of all things—pigeons. Nixalite consists of 2 and 4 foot long metal strips with 120 needle-sharp points protruding from the strips covering a 180 degree radius. The strips, which are 1/4 inch wide, and the points are constructed of 302 stainless steel.

The metal strips can be bent and shaped to conform with any surface you want to prevent squirrels from reaching.

Once installed, Nixalite doesn't need to be maintained. The points remain sharp and the steel won't rust. Should you decide to move the strips, they can be easily repositioned. Because the strips are pliable, you can use Nixalite for a variety of feeder conditions.

Nixalite looks frightening and formidable. As you approach a Nixalite-covered feeder, the spines which spin off in all directions seem to curve toward your skin. Your imagination conjures drops of blood on the Nixalite's tips; you can hear screams emerging from it. Of all the weapons in the anti-squirrel arsenal, Nixalite is the one that makes you—and the squirrel—afraid. Squirrels may not have the intelligence of humans (yes, that's a proven fact), but they recognize Nixalite's dangers.

Nixalite works, that's for sure. But you have to ask yourself whether you're willing to live with a fortress-looking feeder.

Nixalite has another important quality. Used correctly, it won't harm squirrels (or birds). Nixalite's construction prevents animals from crawling across or over it, because they are unable to find any secure footing in the area covered by Nixalite. Nixalite is not designed to trap squirrels; it's not designed to entangle them; it's not designed to stick into squirrels. The spines are angled so that squirrels avoid Nixalite, rather than try to venture into it. According to the manufacturer, "Nixalite is approved by leading humane and bird societies."

Do not to place Nixalite under the feeder where the squirrel might fall. A squirrel falling onto Nixalite would give you the opportunity to try your squirrel recipe.

Nixalite must be installed strategically to be effective. Properly installed, it can prevent squirrels from alighting *on top* of bird feeders, and keep squirrels from climbing up poles and trees.

Let's look at the on-top-of-feeder application first. One the most enjoyable ways for a squirrel to dine is to crawl into an open feeder, such as an alpine-shaped window feeder, and munch away, sheltered from the elements. If the feeder isn't designed to let a squirrel enter, a squirrel's second preference is to hang from the feeder's roof and eat upside down. (Squirrels don't care whether they eat right side up or upside-down. Indeed, squirrels would have made terrific experimental animals for the early days of the space program. Now that's an idea!)

To prevent a squirrel from entering an open-faced feeder, thoroughly cover the top *and* sides of the feeder with Nixalite. Nixalite should also extend over the front of the feeder to prevent the squirrel from using any surface as a platform. It's a good idea, also, to let the Nixalite stretch beyond the feeder's edges, so that there is absolutely no surface the squirrel will want to put its little paws on—no matter how hungry he becomes. There's a correlation between how terrifying your feeder looks and how successful the Nixalite is at keeping out squirrels. As you safeguard your feeder, you should have a fortress mentality.

To discourage squirrels from poaching by hanging upside down, as they like to do from baffles and tube feeders, just place the

Nixalite so that the squirrels can't grip the part of the baffle or feeder they prefer. This means you may have to spend considerable time observing squirrels. Notice *all* the positions they grab. The Nixalite manual points out, "Installation must be handled with ingenuity and skill, so take your time . . . Effective installations don't just happen—they are planned." And remember, squirrels are tenacious: once you block a particular position, they will struggle (and often succeed) at finding another place to hold on to.

Make sure you use enough Nixalite. Too little, and the squirrels will simply go around it.

Nixalite comes with metal fasteners which you can use to secure the strips to your feeder or pole. Alternatively, you can glue the Nixalite on, or use copper bell wire to hold it in position. Household cement works better than superglue, which seems to be helpful only if you want to attach Nixalite to your fingers. (Never use string to secure Nixalite. Squirrels will munch through string.)

Nixalite is most useful when you want to stop a squirrel from climbing a pole or tree. Despite their natural climbing and leaping abilities, squirrels do have to contend with gravity, and Nixalite magnifies gravity's effects on squirrels. As you lay out Nixalite, keep in mind that squirrels have great leaping ability. According to Marie Gellerstedt, president of Nixalite, "the first row must be at least four feet off the ground," otherwise squirrels can leap over it. Gellerstedt pointed out that when squirrels in her yard are being chased by her dog they can jump ten feet with a running start. Attach four or five rows of Nixalite around the circumference of the tree or pole, the first about four feet from the ground, then three or more at five inch intervals. *Do not* wrap Nixalite around the tree or pole barber pole style, because squirrels can grab hold and climb up the spiral. For the same reason, don't arrange Nixalite horizontally. If installed correctly, the squirrels will never reach your feeder by climbing up.

Currently, Nixalite starter kits, consisting of four strips and fasteners, costs $41, which includes postage. Nixalite is available only from the manufacturer, which is listed in Resources.

Perrier Bottles   You ask, how can Perrier bottle stop squirrels from raiding feeders? Mere water, how can that succeed? Well, in special circumstances, Perrier bottles can prevent squirrels from getting to the spots they must launch from to reach your feeder. When leaping, squirrels need to launch themselves from particular angles. This is especially true when their target area for landing is small. Perrier bottles are especially useful when you have to position your feeder close to the ground or other surface such as a window ledge or air conditioner.

Perrier bottles work, but as with most passive anti-squirrel devices, you have to apply the bottles intelligently. Before you position the bottles, pay attention to the locations the squirrel leaps from. After drinking the 99-cent water in the bottle, fill the Perrier bottles with free tap water and bunch them close together to cover the launching area. You must fill the bottles with water, otherwise Mr. Squirrel will easily knock them over. It's best if you glue the bottles together so that the squirrel will be unable to push any one of them over. Alternatively, wrap copper bell wire around the bottles. You'll need at least five bottles.

Squirrels cannot climb Perrier bottles and can't walk on top of them. The surface formed by the bottle tops contains too much empty space for them to find solid footing. No matter how much they paw at the bottles, they won't be able to get on top. For all practical purposes, you've created an area in which squirrels cannot enter—a squirrel-free zone.

Still, the persistent and knowledgeable squirrel may be able to thwart the Perrier system. Such squirrels know that although their preferred launching area is no longer available to them, they can still leap up, and although they won't land in the feeder squirrels may be able to get close enough to reach some part of the feeder, grab hold, and crawl inside. This is known as the close-enough phenomenon. If the squirrel can land on top of the feeder, or reach a chain, perch or other structure . . . well, you've lost. If this occurs, you may need combine Perrier bottles with Nixalite or grease to make life more difficult for the squirrels.

The Squirrel-Proof Habitat

Lola Oberman of Bethesda, Maryland developed a virtually squirrel-proof bird habitat. She enclosed her feeder in a wire mesh box measuring six feet high by four feet on the length and width. The mesh was comprised of two-inch-wide holes—too small for any squirrel to penetrate, but large enough for most birds to get inside. The habitat worked perfectly.

You can construct an anti-squirrel habitat with chicken wire, rubber-coated wire, or any similar mesh wire. Be sure to enclose the top, or squirrels will certainly climb in. Once constructed, you can place the feeder on a pole inside the habitat, or, probably more easily, suspend it from the top. With wire clippers you can construct a door to let you fill the feeder easily. If you're truly adventurous, you can construct an even larger habitat, and fill it with several feeders and a birdbath.

Woodpeckers "Huh? Woodpeckers?" you ask. "How can woodpeckers be used as a defense against squirrels?" Well, to tell you the truth, I'm not exactly sure myself, but it appears that certain woodpeckers have it in for squirrels. According to *Animals of the World*,

> One determined woodpecker will sometimes send a Gray Squirrel scampering after a few moments, for the blows from that long sharp bill of his are severe (p. 165).

Although I know no one who's tried this technique, you might encourage red-headed woodpeckers to visit your yard. You'll either have to figure out what red heads like to eat most, or capture a few and transport them to your area. Who knows, in a little while, red-headed woodpeckers might be sold in birdfeeder catalogs along with baffles and the squirrel-spooker pole.

Baffles Baffling poles is a popular way of trying to thwart squirrels in their attempts to misappropriate bird feed. Baffles work—in theory—by creating a ledge that squirrels cannot climb around. In theory. It's like in the movies where the hero is in great peril because he is unable to climb up and over the rock ledge that extends out from the mountain. But in the movies, the hero manages to gather the energy, courage, and imagination—somehow—to get around that ledge.

Squirrels must watch the same movies, because baffles seem to provide only limited protection against squirrels. The primary way squirrels defeat baffles, according to George Petrides of the Wild Bird Center in Cabin John, Maryland, is by chewing and clawing at the surface and edges of the feeder, roughening it enough so they can grip it and pull themselves over.

There are a couple of techniques you can use to make baffles more effective. First, use the largest baffle you can find. And I mean the absolute largest. It should dwarf whatever feeder lies beneath. A gigantic baffle ensures that squirrels cannot crawl to the edge of the baffle, swing it, and catch on to the feeder below with their paws. Second, draw the feeder high up into the baffle. The more the feeder is near or "in" the baffle, the more difficult it will be for squirrels to jump down and in from the baffle. Third, let the baffle dangle precariously on the wire or chain it's hanging from. The more off-center the baffle's balance, the more likely squirrels are to lose their balance. And fall.

Notice how squirrels use baffles. To keep from falling off, squirrels hang on to the chains, wires, or loops on the top of baffles with their back claws. They need that chain to support themselves while they try to maneuver from the top of the baffle to your feeder.

Fourth, you can add to the baffle's ability to protect your feeder by making it, from the squirrel's perspective, a more complex surface. Build a super-baffle: by gluing a cone to the top of the baffle, it becomes difficult for squirrels to get on top of the baffle at all, because squirrels will have nothing to attach their back claws to.

Cone-shaped super-baffles can be constructed out of Plexiglas or aluminum; the latter is probably easier to make into a cone. The cone should be about 12 inches high and completely surround the chain. It must be as seamless as possible, or squirrels will have something to grip on to.

The cone looks like a "Coolie hat," according to Hoit Palmer of Gaithersberg, Maryland, who developed this system. "Squirrels can see the seed underneath the baffle," she said, describing how it works. "They aim for the seed, then decide to climb the tree, climb across the branch toward the Coolie hat. Then the fun begins." Some squirrels, "especially the older ones," Palmer points out, can stretch far and defeat the Coolie hat by holding on the to chain and letting gravity stretch their body, but "new squirrels can't stretch as far."

In the same vein, you can attach Nixalite to the baffle's top to make that area undesirable for squirrels. Glue Nixalite to the top of the baffle. Be sure to completely cover the baffle's top or squirrels will find a way to grasp the Nixalite and use it to their advantage.

Rating the general effectiveness baffles is difficult. In some situations baffles provide excellent anti-squirrel protection, especially if you are fortunate to live in an area with dumber-than-normal squirrels. (With certain feeders, a baffle will also protect your feeder from less desirable birds, such as starlings.) In other locales, baffles only make squirrels work harder to get their food, and, as a result, make them hungrier when they get to it. Baffles are fairly unattractive, but fortunately don't obscure your view of birds. They also protect feeders from rain and snow, helping to keep birdseed dry.

If your feeder has a built-in baffle, such as the GSP or Mandarin, you don't need a baffle; but for most feeders they're a good idea.

Window Brackets Any time you hang a feeder from a tree you have to deal with squirrels in their natural element. More often than not, if it's possible to hang the feeder from a tree it's possible for the squirrel to get to it. This axiom has something to do with the close working relationship squirrels have to trees—they know how to use them a lot better than you do.

People choose window brackets because they have no alternative. Pole feeders may not be viable for an individual's particular situation. If you don't have a yard, for example, you may need to convince your neighbors that it's okay to put the feeder in the middle of the street. Good luck. Or you may not like the look of a pole on your lawn, may not be crazy about sunflower debris destroying the grass underneath the feeder, or may not like mowing around the pole.

Window feeders aren't always practical either. They can interfere with opening the window, which may be a problem in the summer. Window feeders fall off from time to time—not pleasant if you live in an apartment building and have to run down seven flights of stairs to retrieve the feeder. And window feeders may easily be encroached on by squirrels.

The solution, then, may be a pivoting arm, a steel pole that attaches to a wall and extends out several feet from that wall. Pivoting brackets come in two sizes, 24" and 48". The bracket can be attached to the side of a window, a fence, or any wooden or brick surface. It can be pivoted at various angles from the wall. The bracket attaches to the wall with wood screws, which is easy to do if you're putting it on a fence, and very difficult if you're putting it on the side of an apartment building. To attach it to the side of an apartment building you need 1) to lean out the window and turn the screws tightly, and 2) have no fear of heights. Although wood screws aren't designed to fasten to brick, you can force them, but you may have to reinforce the screws with epoxy to ensure that the bracket stays in place. Because you can attach almost any kind of feeder to a pivoting bracket, it's worth the struggle—and fright—to put one up. (Masonry bits will bore through brick; anytime you drill into the side of a building make sure to get the landlord's permission first.)

As I mentioned, brackets come in two sizes: two feet and four feet. The two foot bracket is practically useless in preventing squirrels from getting to your feeder, especially on apartment buildings: the width of the feeder shortens the distance between the wall and the feeder, and frequently all a squirrel has to do is grab onto the wall or fence with his back claws and stretch. If you must use a 24-inch bracket, attach it to the top part of a fence or above a window so that it extends up into the air. Then the squirrel can't just reach directly out and grab it. Also consider using a narrow tube feeder so that squirrels have to reach farther to grab the feeder. Remember, once they get ahold of the feeder they can pull themselves onto it. Remember also to put a baffle on top of whatever feeder you attach to the bracket, because squirrels can run up the arm with the greatest of ease. In apartments, avoid placing the bracket near a window screen—squirrels can easily climb up screens. Glass, on the other hand, foils squirrels every time.

The four-foot bracket give you added distance between the wall or fence, and the feeder. It's not a foolproof system, and it may be a good idea to coat the bracket with teflon and put Nixalite on the top of your feeder.

Pulleys Sold in your favorite hardware store is an elegant apparatus that can stop squirrels: the pulley. A pulley enables you to place a feeder in remote locations, such as under an eave, between two distant trees, or between a house and a tree. The pulley lets you place feeders in locations that both you and squirrels have a lot of trouble reaching. Once set up, you just have to tug on a the rope to retrieve the feeder to refill it, and tug again to put the feeder back in its squirrel-proof place. There's no universal best place to locate your feeder, so you'll have to improvise.

35mm Film Cans Just about everything can become an anti-squirrel device, 35mm film containers included. Marlene Couture of the Duncraft Company suggests suggests using film containers when you hang your feeder from a line that's stretched between two trees (or a tree and a pole). Punch holes in the bottom of the film containers and string between six and twelve containers through the line on either side of the feeder, just as you might string popcorn. When the squirrels reach the film containers the containers revolve around the string, and the squirrels lose their footing and fall.

Record Albums Record albums are also a successful tool in the arsenal against squirrels, especially 33 rpms, for feeders that are hung from wires strung between two trees. Before you complete the connection between the trees, string the cord through several albums on either side of the feeder. As long as the feeder and wire are high enough so that squirrels can't reach them by jumping, you should have a fairly impenetrable barrier. Squirrels are going to have a difficult time getting over and around the albums. They may be angry with you, but they won't get access to the birdseed. Some people say that Frank Sinatra albums work best, but field surveys have discovered that any plastic album works fine. Needless to add, you shouldn't plan to play those albums again.

Sleds For those bird feeders whose children are passing into adulthood, there are a couple of toys that can be recycled into anti-squirrel devices. Among the most common—in the northern states—and easiest to employ is the metal sledding saucer. If you've ever gone sledding with your kids you *know* how hard it is to stay on one; if you have that much trouble just imagine what a squirrel's going to go through. A sledding saucer makes a terrific baffle, particularly because it's so large and so precariously constructed.

Squirrel Spooker Pole The squirrel spooker pole consists of a pole with a movable sleeve that encases the pole. The sleeve, located near the top of the pole, is designed so that when a squirrel grabs it, the squirrel's weight causes it to slide down. A counterweight brings the sleeve back to its original position. Every time a squirrel tries to climb the squirrel spooker pole, he falls to the ground. Tube and flat bottom feeders can be easily mounted on the pole.

The squirrel spooker pole isn't foolproof, however. In every yard there's probably one squirrel who's figured out the system and has beaten it—by climbing faster than the sleeve slides. You can enhance the pole's ability to thwart squirrels by baffling above and below the feeder and by greasing the sleeve section of the pole. Although not 100 percent effective, the spooker pole gives you an edge over a regular pole.

If there was ever any doubt about the cleverness of squirrels, how some squirrels overcome the Squirrel Spooker pole will destroy that doubt. Peg and Paul Finn of Bedford, New Hampshire said this about their experience with the Squirrel Spooker Pole:

> We no sooner had a feeder attached to the top of the pole when along came Mr. Squirrel. Up the pole he climbed, clawed onto the sleeve, and down he came. We thought that was about the slickest thing we had ever seen and were in hysterics watching as three more attemps were made all ending with the perplexed squirrel on the ground.
>
> Five minutes later he was back with a friend. They both sat under the feeder chatting and looking up. Mr. Squirrel demonstrated one more time while his partner took notes.
>
> As Mr. Squirrel was lowered to the ground he did not release his hold on the sleeve. Instead he held it in place at the bottom of the pole and his partner then climbed up the pole to the feeder without any problem. After which they reversed positions until they both had their fill.
>
> Each day was the same routine—a two squirrel team would arrive, one to hold and one to eat.

Chemical Warfare It may sound awful, but it hasn't been proscribed by the Geneva Convention or the ASPCA, so chemical weapons are allowed in your arsenal against squirrels. Coating the surfaces of the feeder with Ben-Gay, cayenne pepper, or menthol cream will encourage squirrels to attack another feeder. In many instances you can use chemicals in the same place you would apply oil or teflon. Squirrels hate the smell, texture and taste of these substances. They will still work at attacking your feeder, but they will scrupulously avoid coming into contact with the noxious material. Ben-Gay and menthol come in creams so they can be readily applied; cayenne pepper is available in various liquids in the spice department of your supermarket. Asian speciality food stores sell several different kinds of hot pepper sauces. Red pepper mixed with epoxy makes a fine deterrent and is actually used with radio transmitters placed on squirrels so they won't chew the electronics. Vaseline and red pepper works, too. You may have to experiment a little to find the best substance for your particular brand of squirrel. Birds don't like these materials either, but they can fly around them.

Avoid using ammonia. It doesn't keep squirrels away and it makes your yard smell like the New Jersey Turnpike.

PART II: ACTIVE ANIT-SQUIRREL MEASURES

Finally, of course, they won. I came out one morning and saw that the feeders had been knocked down and were nowhere in sight. I found them later; the squirrels had hidden them in the ivy.

Mary McGrory, *Washington Post*

Moving Squirrels It's the scheme of last resort and it is the most effective: moving squirrels. Transporting squirrels isn't too difficult either—just bait a trap with peanut butter, leave the trap out for ten seconds, and voila, there's a squirrel. Then move the squirrel several miles and that squirrel won't be around to bother you any more.

Although that's just about all you have to do to evict squirrels from your property, there are some tips you should follow to make the task easier and safer. First, never stick your finger inside the cage after you've trapped a squirrel. Remember, the squirrel entered the cage to get a bite to eat, and if you put your finger within striking range, that's exactly what it is going to do. If you think you can pull your finger out before the squirrel gets to it, just remember this: you thought you could keep that squirrel away from your birdfeeder in the first place. Thick gloves are a good idea when moving squirrels.

Where you relocate the squirrel is important for several reasons. A distance of *at least* two miles is crucial if you don't want that squirrel to return. Farther is better, and very far—ten miles—is best, because that squirrel may beget baby squirrels who will leave their range in search of food and return to your property. A typical squirrel has a range of between one to seven acres; but we know that your squirrel isn't typical. So unless you move that squirrel a considerable distance, you may find yourself confronting her children in a season or two. Placing barriers between you and where you move the squirrel is a good idea. Superhighways work best, but if you can't get one constructed, fast-moving rivers (remember, squirrels can swim), open areas (squirrels don't tread too far away from trees), rocky areas, houses with cats, a zoo, and a couple of shopping malls will do the trick.

Because you're taking the trouble to move a squirrel rather than convert it into squirrel stew, you probably care what happens to that squirrel. The health and happiness of the squirrel, once you move it, depends entirely on you. Do not put the squirrel where there are plenty of other squirrels, although this may run counter to common sense. An area with plenty of squirrels probably is at its peak carrying capacity, or even beyond it. The newcomer will have to establish her position, or be banished. When there are too many squirrels in a given area, some squirrels must be dislocated. Because squirrel ranges overlap, your ex-squirrel will then shift into another range where she will have to establish herself or again be banished. Remember, the squirrel you've just moved has led a cushy life thanks to your generous feeder and probably won't be as assertive as "wild" squirrels. There are a couple of exceptions to this rule, however. City parks in which people feed the squirrels may be okay for transported squirrels. Many parks, such as Washington's Lafayette Park, contain 6 times the number of squirrels that they would be able to support if no one fed them. The same goes for the White House lawn, where squirrels are fed by members of all political parties. The other exception is during hunting season. Although it may not be wise to wander around carrying an animal in your hand during hunting season, hunting depletes the squirrel population; by transporting a squirrel to a populated range you are actually helping the species.

After you capture the squirrel, move it as quickly as possible. Squirrels do not like to be kept in small cages and will let you know. If they become too upset, squirrels can go into shock and die. When in shock their body temperature drops, and their heart rate either increases or decreases markedly. Be sure to put newspaper or some other material between the trap and the floor of your car—squirrels have several ways of expressing their displeasure. Don't leave the squirrel cooped up too long without water, and don't leave the squirrel in your car with the windows rolled up because your car will become so hot that the squirrel will bake. Check your traps several times a day, and especially around nightfall to make sure that squirrels aren't left inside for long periods. For good measure, cover the trap; it gives the squirrel a sense of security.

Peanut butter is the best bait. It's easy to apply and the smell attracts squirrels from great distances.

Not every trap will do. Hav-a-Hart and Tomahawk Live traps catch squirrels safely and humanely for relocation. Squirrels wander in through a spring-activated door that opens forward and downward under their weight. The door can only be opened from the entrance side, so once inside there is no escape. Be sure to use the correct-size trap. If the trap is too large, the squirrel may escape. Traps are, of course, reusable, and cost about $20. Many local conservation organizations rent traps, too.

It can take a while to trap squirrels, according to Joe Bartelme, who lives in Westchester, New York. He wrote:

> There were cages in the patio, cages on the balcony, under the big spruce, near the woodpile. After five days the catch included a raccoon, the neighbor's cat and two squirrels. But not my squirrels. The overhead morning aerobics continued.

It took Mr. Bartelme so long to get rid of one squirrel that he had named him. When he finally caught Henry, Bartelme had a horrible premonition:

> Just the other day I was driving Henry to his new home, a park in Greenwich, when I noticed a gray, unmarked van approaching in the opposite direction. We did not acknowledge one another. But I am certain, positively

certain, that in the back of that gray, unmarked van were countless cages of Connecticut squirrels, eagerly awaiting their destination in my backyard (from "In Wily Pursuit of Squirrels," Joe Bartelme, the *New York Times*, June 30, 1985. Reprinted by permission).

Dart Guns
I know what you're thinking and I want to tell all the animal welfare people out there that dart guns are entirely harmless to squirrels. In fact, you chances of hitting a squirrel with a dart gun are pretty slim.

So why bother to talk about dart guns as an anti-squirrel weapon? Well, everyone who attempts to thwart squirrels will eventually think of dart guns, so I might as well dispel some myths about them. If you're tempted to buy a rubber-tipped dart gun because you remember the pain you suffered—or inflicted—when using one as a kid, you'll be surprised to discover that squirrels virtually ignore being hit. I blasted one at point blank range and it didn't even seem to know it had been shot.

If you can't discourage squirrels with dart guns, why bother? There's no really good reason, so here are some fair reasons: while you can't hurt them, squirrels aren't crazy about these darts. They'd rather you didn't. Second, it improves your aim, speed, and timing for other anti-squirrel measures. Finally, it gives you something to do other than yell and flail your arms: it's easier on the neighbors.

There's only one thing your should know about dart guns (other than don't aim the gun at your little sister). Don't remove the little red tips from the darts. If you remove the red rubber tips you still won't be able to hurt the squirrels, but you most certainly will not be able to find the darts on the ground.

Robots
One advantage you have over squirrels is technology. Squirrels may be masters of speed, dexterity, and acrobatics and have sharp teeth, but you have the technological edge over them. I'm not talking about hundred thousand dollar laser systems, though that isn't a bad idea; several inexpensive high-tech devices are available for the price of a new birdfeeder (which you may have to buy if you can't get rid of these squirrels).

To recognize which devices are the most appropriate, you have to see the world from a squirrel's perspective. To squirrels everything is large. Other creatures for which the world is large include, of course, birds and children. Toy robots look gigantic to squirrels and small children. Look for anti-squirrel robots at toy stores and Radio Shack. Countless toys designed for little boys simulate weapons of war firing all sorts of missiles. A toy tank won't make a 220-pound man wince, but a 1½ pound squirrel has to take this "weapon" seriously.

The best kind of anti-squirrel toys are remote-controlled ones–robots–because squirrels aren't going to let you get close to them. Some robots are remote-controlled by wire, others by radio—the latter is best.

In addition to tanks, there are a large variety of robots that can work against squirrels, including radio-controlled planes with which you can "buzz" squirrels as they try to escape by running over telephone lines. Think war and you'll do all right.

Some of the best robots are the "mechanical claws". These robot-toys were designed to let kids pretend they are scientists and are remotely operating a "hand" that holds dangerous material. The hand is attached to a arm that can rotate around almost a full 360°. Some of these mechanical claws come on robots with wheels and can travel about.

The best way to use these kinds of robots, the claws, is to leave them on the ground near your birdfeeder. Sprinkle a couple of nuts near the robot. As the squirrel approaches, instruct the robot to grab the squirrel. These robots make excellent feeder guards.

Squirrel Diverters

The most effective anti-squirrel measure is a squirrel diverter. It is also the simplest. Squirrel diverters are actually squirrel feeders. Filled with sunflower seeds, peanuts, and peanut butter, they keep squirrels happy, fed, and most important, away from your feeder. (Some people feed squirrels not just to keep them out of their birdfeeder, but because they **like** squirrels. See Chapter 8.) There are only four points to keep in mind when using a squirrel diverter. First, make it easy for the squirrels to get the seed. Squirrels are notoriously lazy and are attracted to whichever feeder is easier to eat from. Platform feeders work best as squirrel diverters; the Cardinal Barn and other feeders with openings on the bottom work well when placed on the ground. The second point to remember is to keep the diverter as far away from your birdfeeder as possible. You want to remove temptation.

Third, keep the squirrel feeder full. If empty, squirrels will go back to doing what they do best—attacking your feeder. Finally, don't relax your squirrel defenses. Make your feeders as difficult for squirrels to break into as possible. Food is food to squirrels, and some will attempt to reach your feeder no matter what you do.

Diverters are a necessity if you have a hand-made, designer feeder. Any feeder that you want to protect from being mauled and chewed by squirrels must be accompanied by a diverter.

Camera Flashes and Noise These are only temporary measures. Firing flashes and making noise will momentarily stun or scare squirrels (and your neighbors, depending on the hour) but over the long run they won't keep squirrels away. A flash will blind a squirrel for a handful of seconds, giving you enough time to aim and fire a dart gun. These methods will help you relieve your frustrations.

The scorecard kept at The Wild Bird Center in Cabin John, Maryland.

7

101 Cunning Stratagems

"About the only mammals it is impossible to avoid feeding are the squirrels that get into bird feeders."

New York Times

Finally, 101 cunning stratagems to reduce dramatically the egregious misappropriation of seed from your birdfeeder by squirrels. Some of these stratagems will be more useful than others for your particular environment. Good luck.

1. Hang your feeder from a tree. Make sure the feeder is eight feet away from the nearest branch, at least six feet off the ground, and completely covered with a baffle.

2. Dig a moat around your feeder. Fill it with piranha.

3. Fill your feeder with marbles and buy a parakeet to keep indoors.

4. Rent a guard cat.

5. Play Frank Sinatra songs on outdoor speakers, very loudly.

A metal skirt around a tree can prevent squirrels from climbing to your feeder, and keep cats from reaching bird houses.

6. Tame a very strong, fast squirrel; give it plenty of food and teach it to keep other squirrels away.

7. Never sleep, never play, only send out for food—and maintain a constant vigil at your feeders.

8. Read this book to the squirrels so that they understand who's in charge.

9. Fire camera flashes at them.

10. Bury rubber acorns—confuse and confound them.

11. Move to Antarctica and enjoy watching penguins.

12. Move to southern Florida and enjoy flamingos.

13. Paint your feeders to look like owl habitats.

14. Trap them and send them to Antarctica.

15. Convince your neighbors that squirrels are cute and that the neighbors should feed them.

16. Let the Pentagon practice their Star Wars technology on the squirrels in your backyard.

17. Make your yard into a mirror maze.

18. Place a highway through your yard.

19. Electrify your feeder.

20. Construct a customized anti-squirrel robot.

21. Capture the squirrels, dress them in deer costumes, and release them during hunting season. Alternatively, paint the word "DEER" on their sides.

22. Dig deep trap-holes in the ground, and cover them with straw.

23. Encourage your neighbor to take in stray cats.

24. Take up falconry and keep the falcon untethered.

25. Breed aggressive, sterile squirrels.

26. Contact a genetic engineering firm and introduce a gene that changes squirrels' appetites to a preference for mosquitoes.

27. Coat your birdfeeder with chewing gum. That'll teach 'em.

28. Encourage your friends and neighbors to buy squirrel coats.

29. Place two half-sphere baffles around your hanging feeder, one above and one below. Leave a 1″ opening for chickadees.

30. Run outside yelling and waving your arms every time a squirrel appears. Not only will you scare squirrels away, but you will get terrific exercise. (Before attempting this technique, check your local noise ordinances.)

31. Put your feeder on a pole and place that pole in the middle of a swimming pool. If you don't have a pool, dig an artificial lake.

32. Use a window feeder, making sure that there is at least 4 feet of window around the feeder and that the feeder has a roof.

33. Enclose your yard with a 20′ tall Plexiglas fence.

34. On the off-chance that stratagem #33 fails, add a top to that fence. Angle the top up 45° and leave an opening for birds to fly into. If you have trouble with birds flying into the clear fence, paint it with stripes.

35. Capture squirrels and move them to your neighborhood dog run.

36. Tell your neighborhood butcher that you've discovered a cheap supply of meat. Tell him that he can call it chicken and nobody will know the difference.

37. Rattlesnakes are a major predator of squirrels. Acquire some for your lawn. (They also help keep solicitors away.)

38. Dig up their nuts during the winter.

39. Put a truck horn next to your feeder and use it whenever a squirrel appears.

40. Hang your feeder 100 feet down from a 200 foot tall tree.

41. Buy a squirrel puppet. Parade around your yard wearing the puppet. Squirrels can't figure out what in the world is going on and it drives them away.

42. Install a windmill generator in your yard. When it's off put corn cobs on the ends of the windmill arms. Wait for a windy day, and when the squirrels climb on board release the clutch.

43.   Import red squirrels. They're territorial and aggressive. Unfortunately they eat nuts, too.

44.   Import red-headed woodpeckers who will vie with squirrels for nuts.

45.   Import squirrel-eating hawks. (They may, unfortunately, enjoy eating birds, too. If that's the case buy the hawk-proof GSP feeder.)

46.   Import blue jays or mockingbirds; they dislike squirrels.

47.   Place a feeder on top of a pole. Put the pole in the middle of your yard, at least 20 feet away from any tree. Put no less than four baffles beneath the feeder and grease the pole with WD-40 oil.

48.   Put your feeder on a pipe and coat the pipe with vaseline. Wrote George Dye to Audubon's *Naturalist News:* "I watched one venturesome squirrel shinny up the pipe until he hit vaseline. He was surprised, and I was highly amused to see him hit the dirt. Now I vaseline the pipe all the way to the ground. The squirrel smells the pipe and leaves."

49.   Feed birth control pills to squirrels. The city of Venice uses birth control pills for pigeons, so they probably can be made for squirrels, too.

50.   Place a giant Clint Eastwood poster in your yard.

51.   Use radar-tracking laser-sighted guns. Originally designed for the Department of Defense, a handful of these may be available on the black market for $265,000 a piece.

52.   Try sonic rodent repellers. Sold in catalogs, these devices are supposed to repel mice and other rodents by emitting a peculiar ultrasonic sound. You may have to boost the power to make it effective against squirrels.

53.   Record squirrel warning sounds on a continuous loop tape and play them over and over again.

54. Practice hitting squirrels with golf balls. Your chances of making successful contact are about 1 in three billion, but your golf swing will improve.

55. Reprogram Soviet ICBM computers to target your back yard. Initiate an action that starts World War III. (This is an extreme measure, but it's guaranteed to eliminate your squirrel problem.)

56. Leak the news that your back yard is a training ground for Contra rebels.

57. Invite Fred the Furrier over to your house to "take care" of your problem.

58. Build a special cannon/gun. It'll be about 10 feet long and 6 inches wide and will fire cats. Aim this cat-gun directly at squirrels.

59. Feed the squirrels caramel apples. They'll love them, but won't be able to open their mouths for days afterwards.

60. Buy some lasers and set up a hologram show in your yard. Make holograms of cats and hunters.

61. Hire a hypnotist to modify squirrels' minds so that they no longer desire nuts, or think they're geckos.

62. Make use of patent #4,712,512, awarded on December 15, 1987 for a birdfeeder made from a plastic bottle, invented by Bernhard Schreib. Here's the patent as described by Mr. Schreib: A method and apparatus components for converting a plastic carbonated beverage bottle into a bird feeder. The apparatus components include pointed feeder trays for insertion into the bottle through specially formed slots cut in the sidewall of the bottle, and a decorative sleeve with corresponding cut-outs is secured around the bottle sidewall. An umbrella-like cover made from a flat piece of flexible plastic is clamped atop the bottle by the bottle closure cap of the bottle to protect the seed from rain and to prevent squirrels and the like from taking the bird seed. A piercing-and-cutting tool is provided to pierce the bottle sidewall and sleeve to create the slots for the insertion of the feeder trays and is also useful for making an opening in the bottle cap for the receipt of a support line. A reinforcing cap washer is nested interiorly of the bottle closure cap for added strength and attachment with the support line. A support hook is provided for connection to the support line and for the support of the bird feeder made by the apparatus and method steps.

63. Employ patent #4,637,164 for a squirrel guard by inventor Harold O. Brown:

An animal guard for tree trunks comprising an annular flexible plate having a central circular opening and a skirt portion completely around the central opening; at least one slot extending through the skirt forming the plate into a separable member having abutting edges; a pair of spaced fastener holes in the skirt radially aligned and positioned adjacent one abutting edge of the slot; an inner and an outer spaced parallel arcuate slot in the skirt radially spaced from one another and positioned so that the fastener holes and the slots cooperate with each other when the plate is positioned in a truncated conical position about a tree trunk; the inner slot and associated fastener hole being a substantial distance closer to the inner periphery of the plate than the outer slot and associated fastener hole is to the outer periphery so as to not provide a gripping surface for an animal attempting to pass the guard.

64. Employ patent #4,541,362, a squirrel-proof selective bird feeder, invented by Allan W. Dehls of Bridgewater, New Hampshire:

A squirrel-proof selective bird feeder includes a metallic hopper having integral side walls and a back wall defining an open front face, an open top, and a feed portal, a translucent window fastened in water-resistant sealing engagement to the open front face, a top having a sandwiched metallic plate slidably mounted in and frictionally retained by the confronting walls of the open top of the hopper, and a spring-loaded perch having an adjustable tension pivotally mounted to the bottom of the hopper and adjacent the feed portal.

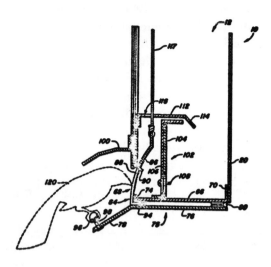

Employ patent # 4,541,362

65. Employ patent #4,523,546 for a squirrel-proof bird feeder, invented by Peter A. Latham of Rye, New Hampshire:
A device for squirrel-proofing bird feeders includes a flexible covering sheet mounted above or to the upper end of the bird feeder. The sheet is dimensioned and located with respect to the feeder so that when a squirrel attempts to walk on the sheet, the sheet will flex and bend downwardly under the influence of the squirrel's weight. The squirrel will slide off the sheet and with no means or opportunity to grab onto any portion of the sheet or the feeder which it covers.

66. Employ patent 4,498,423 for a bird feeder invented by Leon Gainsboro and Peter A. Latham:
A bird feeding device is provided with a perch which can be adjustably positioned with respect to the feeding opening to selectively accommodate different sizes of birds. The perch is movable toward and away from the feeding opening so that for larger birds the perch is positioned farther from the feeding opening than for smaller birds. The disclosed embodiment also includes a simultaneous heightwise adjustment for the position of the perch so that it is lowered when in its more extended position. Also disclosed is an improved arrangement for attaching the perch and feeding device to the container of the bird feeder. Another

aspect of the invention relates to a bird feeder having a storage and feeding tube which is detachably connected to an overhead support by a quick disconnect device which provides for quick and simplified filling of the feed tubes as well as an arrangement which minimizes spilling or loss of bird seed.

67. Employ patent #4,462,337 for a bird feeder with a rotatable cover, invented by Peter Kilham of Foster, Rhode Island:
A bird feeder having a generally planar seed tray and means for mounting such in a generally horizontal position. The bird feeder further includes a cover, generally of dome-shaped configuration and having a lower peripheral edge frictionally supported on an upstanding peripheral seed tray rim. The cover is capable of rotational movement with respect to the tray such that a bird access opening in the cover may be adjustably positioned downwind of the feeder in its use position.

68. Employ patent #4, 434,745 for a bird feeding device, invented by Noel Perkins of Northwood, New Hampshire:
A bird feeding device is disclosed which can be accessed by birds and not by squirrels. The device comprises a container for holding feed and a wire mesh enclosing the container. An O-ring supports the container within the wire mesh and spaces the mesh away from the container such that the mesh is not directly in contact with the container whereby squirrels are prevented from accessing the container.

69. Employ patent #4,389,975, a dual purpose bird feeder invented by James B. Fisher, Jr. of St. Louis, Missouri:
A dual purpose bird feeder for use mounted upon a post with a squirrel baffle preventing climbing upon the feeder or for use in a free hanging relation where it is supported on a chain. The bird feeder is comprised of a frusto-conical hollow feeder housing with a tray at the bottom and flat shallow roof at the top. In the freely supported relation the feeder tray has a radius not exceeding about 55% of the radius of the roof and the outer periphery is positioned underneath the upper portion of the housing. The depth of the tray beneath the roof also does not exceed about one-half of the radius of the roof. This relationship prevents or discourages squirrels or large undesirable birds from using the

feeder tray. In the post supported version the squirrel barrier baffle is of the same frusto-conical construction as the feeder housing for ease in manufacture and is positioned underneath the tray. A cylindrical baffle may depend from the tray to which the frusto-conical baffle may be removably attached. Means are provided for a central post to connect to the feeder. The inverted upwardly flaring baffle and its spacing of the bottom wall from the central support post effectively prevents squirrels from climbing the post on the feeder tray.

Employ any of the following patents:

70. 4,327,669, May 4, 1982, Multiple bird feeder, Morton Blasbalg, Warwick, Rhode Island

71. 4,323,035, Apr. 6, 1982, Squirrel-proof bird feeder, Abraham Piltch, Silver Spring, Maryland

72. 4,188,913, Feb. 19, 1980, Bird feeders, Norman M. Earl and Alexander M. Brown, Stafford Springs, Connecticut and Daytona Beach, Florida respectively

73. 4,171,463, Oct. 16, 1979, Rodent proof cable, David Watkins, Arleta, California

74. 4,031,856, Jun. 28, 1977, Squirrel-proof post, Russell L. Chester, Fontana, Wisconsin

75. 4,030,451, Jun. 21, 1977, Bird feeder, Isobel Miller, Greenville, New Hampshire

76. 3,977,363, Aug. 31, 1976, Bird feeder, James B. Fisher, Jr., St. Louis, Missouri 63124

77. Use the fact that squirrels are either right-handed or left-handed against them. I'm not sure how you can use this to your advantage, but there must be a way.

78. Idea from Bill Avery of Springfield, Virginia: "Feed them unmercifully. Get them so fat that they can no longer sit on the edge of your birdfeeder."

79. Squirrels hate the smell of naphthalene (mothballs).

80. Copper naphthenate in linseed oil is an excellent squirrel repellent.

81. Plant exotic trees, or small-seeded evergreen or deciduous trees such as birch, willow or elms. The squirrels don't go for them.

82. Remove trees that have squirrel dens in them.

83. Follow squirrels as they gather twigs and leaves to build nests. Destroy the nests as they build them.

84. Clean and bone the squirrel. Soak the meat in egg for about 20 minutes. Coat with bread crumbs, oregano, paprika, cumin, and mustard seed. Bake at 400° for forty minutes. Remove from the oven and cover with Cheddar cheese. Continue baking for another ten minutes. Serve with wild rice.

85. Place your feeder on a squirrel spooker pole. Grease the sleeve with oil. Place a baffle beneath and above the feeder. Cover the top and bottom baffles with Nixalite.
That should do it.

86. Attach a motor to a pole. Set the pole to rotate at thirty revolutions a minute. Between the pole and the feeder place a ball bearing so that the feeder stays in place.

87. Try Edward F. Vigezzi's Ziploc bag technique:
Normally the squirrels rummage through the debris on the deck after they attempt to get to the birdhouses. While they are searching, I get a 1-quart Ziploc bag and fill it approximately two thirds with water. After sealing it, I then go upstairs to the third floor guest room and open the window very carefully. I palm the baggy in my hand so that when I throw it, the bag will land on one of the sides. After I get a good angle, I toss the bag at the squirrel below. (You have to make sure the squirrel is not watching you.) When the bag hits, it is a double-whammy. The noise of the impact against the wood, and the wall of water will startle the squirrel

and he will quickly retreat to the woods. Depending on the distance from the squirrel, we will determine the length of time they will stay away. In addition, it leaves the deck wet for the birds to enjoy. You always want to get close, but you should not try to hit them directly.

88. Cry. Maybe the squirrel will feel sorry for you and go away.

89. Buy toy rockets with solid fuel engines—the kind that hobbyists play with. Fire a dozen off from your yard every day. No creature enjoys eating in a space launching center.

90. Kidnap baby squirrels and hold them for ransom.

91. Replace the sunflower seed with plastic seed. The squirrels will become confused and go away; the birds aren't smart enough to be confused and will return as soon as you put regular seed back in your feeder.

92. Place a television and VCR in your yard. Rent and play documentaries of owls and hawks. (Again, the birds are too dumb to be confused by the video.)

93. Go to tree climbing school (see Chapter 8, which talks about a tree climber) and take direct, offensive action against squirrels.

94. Hire a lawyer.

95. Sick the IRS on them.

96. Place a drop of superglue on either side of a peanut. Set in your back yard.

97. Import killer bees.

98. Strip the insulation off the power lines that run through your neighborhood. The next time a squirrel tries to run along the line will be his last time doing that.

99. Place several automatic lawn sprinklers in your yard and run them all the time. Squirrels don't like to come out in downpours.

Mr. Squirrel approaches the coolie hat baffle cautiously. Although his footing is never absolutely secure, the squirrel is absolutely certain that he's going to get to that birdseed. And he does. Photos by Hoit Palmer.

100. Acquire squirrel-essence. Dab the stuff around and hopefully your squirrels will become hopelessly confused.

101. Decide that squirrels aren't so bad after all.

According to Dr. C. Hart Merriam, pre-World War II experiments with squirrels showed:

They were extremely fond of music, and it affected them in a peculiar manner. Some were not only fascinated, but actually spellbound, by the music-box or guitar. And one particularly weak-minded individual was so unrefined in his taste that if I advanced slowly whistling, 'Just before the Battle, Mother,' in as pathetic a tone as I could muster for the occasion, he would permit me even to stroke his back, sometimes expressing his pleasure by making a low purring sound.

When listening to music . . . they sat bolt upright, inclining a little forward (and if eating a nut, were sure to drop it), letting the forepaws hang listlessly over the breast, and, turning the head to one side in a bewildered sort of way, assumed a most idiotic expression (*Animals of the World*, pp.165–166).

8

What To Do If You Think Squirrels Are Cute

There are an increasing number of individuals who view all of this baffle-buying, arm-flailing, water-pistol-firing and general anti-squirrel hysteria as foolish. These bird feeders—yes, bird feeders—adhere to a different school of thought: not outwitting squirrels. They don't bother to bother with squirrels. Although this may appear to be a defeatist attitude, many admirers of this system believe that theirs represents a holistic approach toward wildlife. Birders who believe in feeding squirrels, instead of acting out vengeful fantasies toward them, arrive at this philosophy for several reasons. First, their attitude is that all wildlife should be treated equally. Birds, squirrels, flying squirrels, gazelles—they're all wild creatures and deserve to survive. Second, these birder-squirrelers feel that squirrels are cute too. (There's no coincidence in the fact that many are myopic.) They way they shinny on a branch, their furry faces, the way they scratch their heads with their paws—all of this is fun to watch, they say. Third, these people have usually become exhausted trying to defeat squirrels. They're pooped.

I think we all know that feeling.

Actually, there's nothing wrong with this approach toward squirrels. While not outwitting squirrels may be giving in to the enemy, it can save a lot of time and money, as well as lower your blood pressure. "People who feed birds spend more time feeding and talking about squirrels than they do about birds," said Tom Post of Audubon Workshop. It's only a tiny step further to actually liking feeding squirrels.

Soviet security chief, Mikhail Dokuchayev, fed squirrels on the White House Lawn during Mikhail Gorbachev's visit to Washington in 1988. Photo by Peter Heimsath.

One proponent of this point of view is Dick E. Bird, publisher of the *Dick E. Bird News* (subtitled "The Best BirdStories Ever Told"). Dick E. Bird's real name is Richard Mallory, but all his friends have been calling him Dick E. Bird, so he figured, well, if that's what people call him, that's what he should be called. Currently, he's trying to get his name trademarked.) Dick Bird created the *Dick E. Bird News* as a way of promoting his company's birdhouses. After some time, he decided that publishing the *Dick E. Bird News* was more fun and rewarding than selling houses, so the house business is dwindling, while the *Dick E. Bird News* is becoming more popular. Bird tries to combine pure facts and fun facts in the *Dick E. Bird News*. He devotes considerable attention to squirrels because wherever you find feeders there will be squirrels. Bird says that he could spend even more time writing about squirrels, but birders, he found, do want to read something about birds every once in a while. Bird's considerable expertise with feeding birds and the resultant squirrel problems has led him to a single conclusion: "There isn't anything that's going to keep squirrels away. My philosophy is to feed squirrels and birds and enjoy."

Dick Bird has seen just about every conceivable anti-squirrel measure. "I've heard everything—from baffles to grease. One guy had an electric fence charger hooked up to his feeder so that squirrels got jolted. I had a Droll Yankee feeder that I tested and I thought that there was no way a squirrel could get in. I hooked the feeder part way up high into the baffle. The feeder was hanging on monofilament line far away from any branch so there was no way a squirrel could climb or lean on to it. I watched one squirrel fly down onto the dome and go crashing off onto the ground. Then one day—I don't know how he did it—there was a squirrel sitting inside that feeder.

"Squirrels must have suction cups on their feet."

Bird knows that squirrels aren't smarter than humans. It's just that "What else is there for squirrels to do other than try to break into feeders? The squirrels don't know that you're putting out birdseed for birds. They think it's for them."

There's another advantage to providing food for birds and squirrels. It keeps them from eating birdfeeders. "Basically, as long as a gray squirrel can get the seed he wants, he won't chew on a feeder," Bird observes. "But if he can't get to the seed— he's dynamite. He'll chew through whether it's plastic or metal."

But on this score, Bird does offer some advice. "Ben Gay or hot pepper—apply them when you spot a squirrel starting to chew on your feeder. That stuff will keep them from eating away. But how long it lasts, I don't know."

How do you manage to feed squirrels and birds? "We have a separate feeder for squirrels," says Dick E. Bird. "And in the fall we forage around and collect acorns and other nuts, put them out for squirrels, and the squirrels go crazy. Collecting nuts works well. Squirrels will only find 20 percent of what they bury. The other nuts become lost or trees or something. What we do is provide the squirrels with what they've buried." It's easy to do this, Bird maintains: "A lot of people who feed birds are already into nature and hiking. Foraging works. On one walk you can collect about a bushel of nuts."

You'll find squirrel-lovers just about everywhere you find bird-feeders. They're not as plentiful, but they are as vociferous. Julie Gillisipie of Bethesda, Maryland is one such person. She said about the bravery of her squirrels:

> For five years I have fed a host of birds and an average of 3 to 7 squirrels. I never tried to discourage squirrels and never seem to suffer from them. I instead enjoyed their antics, play, and the remarkable way they trained our three cats. The squirrels fed mainly on the driveway and the cats learned they couldn't catch them, so the squirrels allowed the cats to within three feet.

After the *Wild Bird News* featured an article about *Outwitting Squirrels*, the publisher received a letter from a pro-squirrel person who expressed her sentiments about feeding squirrels. Mildred Raitala's letter sums up how many squirrel lovers feel about thwarting squirrels:

> Dear George,
>
> I am disappointed at Mr. Adler's attitude in regard to squirrels. I have fed and studied birds most of my life—however that does not keep me from buying roasted peanuts, sunflower seed and filberts in season and feeding the squirrels. The only reason they get in the bird feeders is that they are hungry. In the fall of 1987 there was not many acorns. We have cut down so many trees, that squirrels depend on us for food. So why torment these cunning little acrobats by trying to starve them out?
>
> How would Mr. Adler like to be stuck in a snow storm in a tree without a supply of food? If you give them food they will leave the bird feeders alone, as well as the bulbs in the yard.
>
> If I were hungry I would try every means I have available to get food.
>
> Mildred Raitala

Squirrel-lovers offer their friends more than mere affection. When Clarence Shilling died in August 1982 at the age of 78 he left his entire estate of $90,000 for an endowment to feed birds *and* squirrels. Shilling was a retired mathematics professor, who taught at North Dakota State University. Foundation officials said, "He spent many, many days coming up with language to include in his will that would provide a perpetual endowment in Fargo-Moorhead to care for squirrels and birds."

When Good Squirrels Go Bad This is the story of Ken Gorelick, Cheryl Opacinch, and Seymour the Squirrel. It's a story about a couple who befriended a squirrel, became close compatriots of this squirrel, and then suddenly found that this squirrel abused their trust. It's a story about happiness and disappointment. It's a happy story with a sad ending, but one that shows that sometimes you can love a squirrel too much.

Ken Gorelick and Cheryl Opacinch live near the National Zoo in Washington, D.C., an area whose native wildlife consists of squirrels, raccoons, piliated woodpeckers, hawks, orphaned poodles, and escapees from the Zoo. Trees fill the streets, alleys and parks in the area. There's "a stand of maples out back that the squirrels frequent," said Gorelick. A squirrel which Gorelick and Opacinch named Seymour began appearing at the bedroom balcony of their four-story townhouse during the winter about five seasons ago. Long branches from the maples, a telephone wire that comes into their house, and balconies with railings on every floor provided ample access for squirrels.

Gorelick and Opacinch admired Seymour. Not long after he appeared they began supporting his heavy nut habit. It was an-arrangement that benefited both parties: Seymour got his nuts and Gorelick and Opacinch got to see Seymour. "He was a striking squirrel," Gorelick said. "Seymour was large with long fur and a long bushy tail. He would run to the balcony door like he had known us for a long time. Seymour would wait outside, sit on his hind legs, crane his neck, and ask 'Where are the nuts? I know they're here somewhere.' And he was right," Gorelick said in the tone of voice mixed with admiration, love, and bittersweet melancholy. He spoke as if conjuring the words from deep memory. "One of us would have to distract him by tapping on the glass of the window, so he would go in that direction. After we distracted him from the door, we would open the door a crack and toss out the nut," Gorelick continued. "He would thank us and then go off with the nut. Seymour would then come back in a few minutes for another nut. Then he would send over a lady friend and two or three cousins."

Gorelick and Opacinch fed Seymour through the winter. They become fond of him and thought that he was one of the most beautiful squirrels they had ever seen. "This ritual exchange would occur every day. He knew that we were interested in seeing his tail and he would flick it for us. He could fold it right back to the base of his ears. He would flick his tail for us because he knew that we enjoyed it. We developed a relationship."

As summer approached, Gorelick and Opacinch changed their routine slightly. Gorelick said, "In warm weather we tend to leave the glass door open and the screen door shut." From the balcony "Seymour could see the bowl of nuts sitting on the dresser beside the bed" that they would feed him with.

This is when their relationship deteriorated. "Seymour knew that the nuts were his," Gorelick said softly. "One day we failed to show at the regular time. Finding the glass door open, he took it upon himself to come in on his own. He ate his way through the screen door—he gnawed a hole through the metal screen.

"He cleaned out the bowl and exited.

"Seymour didn't get into anything else," Gorelick added, as if defending Seymour from misplaced allegations.

"He didn't think twice about it, I believe. Seymour was back the next day at the usual time. He figured that we wanted him to have those nuts.

"I was very angry," Gorelick reflected. "I would say we had a huge falling out and I never felt the same after that. He could tell. He came around a few more times and I just glowered at him. He came around a few more times and stopped. He just left because he wasn't wanted."

Gorelick's had time to think about what happened between him and Cheryl, and Seymour. Other squirrels have come by, including Seymour's grandsquirrel, Gregory, but "there has never been another Seymour. He was a uniquely gorgeous creature."

Still Gorelick doesn't regret what happened. "I just felt that we could not continue the kind of hospitality that he was growing to expect," Gorelick said.

But Gorelick and Opacinch don't fault Seymour. "I can't blame him really. He just went for his nut bowl. That's why he didn't understand and was hurt. Perhaps I should have explained, but perhaps I couldn't trust him anymore. And he may have felt the same way after I turned on him so viciously.

"It was a classic case of misunderstanding," Gorelick concluded.

Attracting Squirrels Are you kidding? you ask. No, absolutely not. There are plenty of people who like squirrels and want to coax them into their yard, and there are others who've reconciled themselves to the fact that they are going to feed squirrels no matter what. Attracting squirrels is a much easier task than attracting birds; indeed, all you have to do is put out a birdfeeder and squirrels will flock to your house. So why bother to make any extra effort? The reason is that with a little effort you can increase the squirrel's pleasure in dining and your pleasure in watching squirrels.

Some birders prefer that squirrels eat from their birdfeeders, because it's fun to watch squirrels scramble, climb, and stretch to get to them. These people have found that one feeder serves all. That's fine.

Chapter 6 talks about erecting squirrel diverters to keep these mammals away from your feeder. Squirrel diverters have two attributes that make them work. First, they are kept as far away from the birdfeeder as possible, and second, diverters are easy for squirrels to get to. A bowl with sunflower seeds or nuts will work well both as a diverter and as a squirrel feeder. Alternatively, there are plenty of commercial squirrel feeders. The Audubon Workshop, for example, sells a "corn grabber" that's coaxes squirrels to "jump, swing, hang upside down, pull the chains up to themselves and fight for turns." Another product, a Squirrel-a-Whirl, lets squirrels spin on a windmill-like device as they eat.

If you're serious about keeping squirrels in your yard, you'll need two other elements: water and squirrel boxes. For water any birdbath will do. Just remember to clean it regularly. Build a nesting box and the squirrels in your yard will be your friends forever. Squirrels prefer human-made nesting boxes to squirrel-made nests because they are sturdier and offer greater protection from the elements. A nesting box should be about 14 to 16 inches tall, 4 to 6 inches deep, and 4 to 6 inches wide. Make the entrance hole about two inches in diameter and place it about two inches from the top of the box.

Finally, securely fasten the box to a tree, between 1/2 to 2/3 of the way up the tree.

A couple of words of caution, however. As Gorelick and Opacinch learned, befriended squirrels decide that being inside your house is a lot more pleasant than staying outdoors all the time. Don't leave nuts or other food inside where squirrels can see or smell them—they'll get to them, and if you're extra unlucky they will decide that the stuff in your sock drawer makes wonderful nesting material. The second caution is on a slightly more serious note. If you start to handle squirrels or feed them by hand, eventually you will get bitten. As one author noted, the fastest way for a squirrel to get access to a nut is to bite the hand holding it, which then promptly drops the nut. Squirrel bites are not generally serious—although they are painful—if you've had a tetanus vaccination or booster within the past 10 years. As a matter of safety, all biologists who regularly handle squirrels receive boosters. So if you start to get close to squirrels, make sure you get a shot first.

Peter Jenkins and His Pet Squirrel, Mad Max

Not all squirrel stories involve theft, intimidation, and agony. Some people like squirrels. A few have pet squirrels. It's not my purpose to encourage readers to adopt squirrels, nor do I necessarily believe they are "cute pets." But those of us who are firmly in the outwitting squirrels camp can learn a great deal about squirrels from those who have an owner-pet relationship with them. (Even if it's not clear who owns whom.)

Peter Jenkins found Mad Max, a gray squirrel, about four years ago when he was climbing a tree. Jenkins, a tree surgeon and cofounder of Tree Climbers International in Atlanta, Georgia spends a lot of time in trees and comes eye to eye with squirrels on a regular basis.

"Max is a refugee from a dead tree," Jenkins told me. "The deader the tree the more wildlife is in it. A dead tree is easier to carve. Anyway, we were removing a large white oak. I'd climbed up the tree and stripped the branches. While up there I was keeping my eye open for nesting sites. If I come upon an animal's nest, and there's a baby in it, the parents will run away from the nest, but will return later. I will evacuate the babies before I drop the tree." Jenkins always carries a cardboard box with him when he's dropping trees. "If there's a nearby tree, you can get a cardboard box and tack it to the tree. It makes a great new nest."

Jenkins continued with Max's story. "In this case there was no tree to tack a box to." Jenkins had combed the tree carefully. "I didn't know there were any babies in the tree. After the tree hit the ground, I started to cut it up in different sections. About halfway through I heard that pitched whistle. Baby squirrels have a high-pitched distress signal. Buried inside a sawdust pile was a squirrel. This squirrel was about as young as you can find.

"Mad Max still had his umbilical cord. He was about 1¼ inches long. But despite his size, he was yelling his head off."

I asked Jenkins how Max the Squirrel got his name. "I was driving down the freeway with both doors open—it was in the summer, real hot. A semi truck came by. Mad Max was in a cardboard box, and the truck just sucked the box out of the car. I was doing about 55. I ran out and got to the box and Mad Max was still in it. I couldn't believe he was alive. So we call him the Road Warrior" (after the character portrayed by Mel Gibson in the movie, Mad Max).

After some time, "We tried to release him. He literally walked over the neighbors' cat who was snoozing. Mad Max never saw a cat before and wasn't afraid of it."

Jenkins and his wife had to fulfill the role of mother squirrel. They had to prepare a special milk formula ("not cow's milk; it'll kill them") and feed Mad Max every three or four hours. Squirrels in captivity do differ from those in the wild (if you call a bird-feeder-filled back yard "wild.") "Mad Max was raised alone," Jenkins said. If you raise squirrels in pairs they're half wild. Mad Max will chase females a little bit, but he pretty much doesn't pay attention to other squirrels.

"Mad Max is in a cage inside our screened-in front porch. We let him out there. He's gotten completely out several times but always goes back to the screened porch. He's totally uninterested in the wild."

Max is as good a climber as any squirrel, but not as daring. "Mad Max can run up and down trees, but doesn't go up super high."

Max lives well, too. "Mad Max has a steady diet of pecans. We have four pecan trees in the yard. Once in a while he gets almonds. He has a bad addiction to chocolate and we try not to give him too much because it's so rich."

Max isn't perfect, however. "Once and a while he slips in the house. He's always trying to turn the doorknob to get in. If he has a pecan in his mouth, there's no way you're going to catch him. He's in the hiding mode.

"You have to watch him inside. Sometimes he likes to take a bite out of an antique piece of furniture. If you keep him in the house for three or four hours he gets into the mode of having to make a nest. The first place he goes is the kleenex box. He takes some kleenex in his mouth and bunches it up into a wad. Then he runs to a cardboard box. He keeps going back and forth between his box and the kleenex box. It's very funny."

"Mad Max makes clicking sounds. A lot of clicking sounds. Once and a while he scolds when a neighborhood cat comes around, but not too often."

Jenkins has had some close encounters with squirrels in trees. "I was attacked once. When a squirrel reaches adolescent stage, the parents become protective. I was dead wooding a tree" when it happened, said Jenkins. "I had one dead branch left and the branch came out on a nest. I swung over and started cutting. Then I looked, and two yards over saw two parent squirrels in the next tree. They ran down my tree and were gnashing and lunging at me. I started barking at them but it didn't do any good. Then I started swinging my rope to scare them. They backed away and kept scolding me. Then the parents ran to the three adolescents."

Jenkins thinks squirrels are wonderful. "I love squirrels. They are much more intelligent than birds. I don't think they're trainable to do tricks, but Max knows certain things. He knows my tone of voice. If I lower my voice he cowers down. If he bites too hard I hit him on the top of the head with my knuckle—he knows he's bitten me and cowers."

Max knows Jenkins and his wife, but "reacts differently to strangers. When Peter Jenkins comes home, Max will "jump on me and go through my pockets. He likes to hug my elbow. But "he's not good around strangers. I found that out the hard way. He bites. Two or three of my friends were jumped on and bitten.

"Max knows exactly who's who."

"After I've been out trimming and working different trees and I come home, he sniffs and sniffs me. I bring him cut branches from the trees I have been cutting. He'll spend 15 minutes sniffing me."

Jenkins has had time to reflect on squirrel behavior. "Different squirrels have different personalities. I have a friend whose pet squirrel loves french fries. But Max won't touch them."

In the original Norman-French version of the fairy tale Cinderella, her slippers were made of squirrel fur.

Washington, D.C.'s first wild black squirrels were said to be escapees from the National Zoo. Twenty-eight black squirrels from Ontario, Canada were brought to the zoo between 1902 and 1906.

9

The Feline Menace

"It's such a relief to see a squirrel on a 'cat watch,'
while eating its well-earned seed."

Christian Science Monitor

Although this book is entitled *Outwitting Squirrels*, it's not really just about squirrels. *Outwitting Squirrels* is about protecting your birdfeeder from all sorts of enemies: squirrels, anonymous malicious children, pigeons, and cats. Although squirrels are the most annoying and costly pests—one squirrel can consume a pound and a half of birdseed a week—they're not necessarily the most disruptive. That award, of course, belongs to malicious children. Since there's nothing you can do àbout malicious children that aren't yours, let's focus on the second most disruptive pest: cats.

Cats are bad. Very bad. They scare birds from your feeder. Those that they don't scare they kill. Really not good for bird-feeding at all. When a cat kills a bird that you've fed, it's as if you're feeding the cat indirectly. That's not what birding is about. If you wanted to feed cats you would have bought a six-pack of Nine Lives, not five pounds of hulled sunflower seed. Some people say that cats are beneficial because they drive squirrels away, but what's the use if the consequence of this ecology is that the only animals in your back yard are cats?

Two Kinds of Cat Problems There are two kinds of cat problems. The first, called **Type Y**, is your cat. The second kind of cat

159

problem, called **Type N**, is your neighbor's cat. (There's actually a third type of cat, **Type S**, strays, but Type S cats only prowl neighborhoods with mice and I'm sure you don't live in that kind of neighborhood.) Each problem creates its own set of potential solutions. Let's look at the Type Y cat problem first.

Type Y Cat Problems

The Type Y cat is a common element in people's homes, running second only to microwaves as a possession that doesn't let you do anything you couldn't already do. The cat usually appears the weekend after the following is heard: "Daddy, can I have a cat please if I promise to take care of it please can I daddy please okay please?" In the beginning, Type Ys (kittens at that stage) are tolerable, even cute. Sure they mark up the furniture, coat the kitchen floor with kitty litter, like to greet dawn with shrill meows, and confuse your leg with a scratching post. But they are soft and cuddly. Within a few weeks the kittens turn into bigger kittens and then, following nature's plan, turn into cats. Their meows become louder. Their claws become bigger and sharper. Their litter box becomes . . . Their willingness to play when *you* want to diminishes. Their love for the pre-dawn hours accelerates.

Your patience disappears.

So you let the cat out of the house. You're a little nervous at first because the cat could get hit by a car or run away. (Not that running away would be terrible in the abstract, but **you** would be the one assigned to put a fresh set of size Ds in the flashlight and go hunting up and down the street yelling, "Here kitty kitty. Here kitty kitty.") But cats like it outside and who are you to argue with nature?

Until. Until the cat discovers your birdfeeder and launches into its Great Lion routine. Hunter and Protector of The Back Yard. Provider of All. Yes, your cat is generous and faithful, bringing back trophies for you to see and enjoy. What is particularly upsetting (to you) is that the cat is proud and wants to make a big impression; so she deposits the bird on your pillow. If you confront your cat about this and try to discuss the problem in as normal a tone of voice as you can maintain under the circumstances, she gets upset but still brings the birds inside. Peggy Robin, who has owned several cats, discovered that if you scold cats they then hide their captured birds, usually in closets—and not so cleverly—leaving a trail of feathers along the way.

Fortunately there's a simple solution to the Type Y cat dilemma. Keep your cat indoors. This may not be ideal, but as you have already discovered, it's better than having your cat create an indoor dead bird exhibit.

Type N Cats Neighbors' cats are a serious problem and do not lend themselves to simple solutions. Your neighbors are not going to appreciate your suggestion that they keep their cats inside. And you can't keep their cats in your house. You could be arrested for cat-napping. Even worse, everyone will think that you're one of those crazy people who fills his house with cats, and probably has willed his entire estate to them. You can't shoot the cats because that will get your neighbor mad and she may shoot your birds in revenge. (Although there is the possibility that with so many squirrels around your yard she may think squirrels are your pets and shoot them. But that's a risk you have to evaluate for yourself.)

What follows are the options available to you for coping with bird-killing Type N cats. Good luck.

1. Get the cat to wear a bell—it does the trick. You may have trouble convincing your neighbor's cat (or yours) to wear a bell, but in the long run they will appreciate the bell because it increases the challenge of the hunt. Bells are not foolproof, but they do even the odds. Dick E. Bird, publisher of the *Dick E. Bird News*, recommends the heaviest bell possible, such as the Liberty Bell. It keeps them from jumping too high.

   Some cats have learned to defeat bells, however, by pretending to be statues. They lie in the lawn, sometimes under a shrub, and when a bird hops along, they thrust their paws out and poof, no more bird. Birds, it seems never learn about cat statues. (Some people say this is nature's way of removing stupid birds.) Other cats learn to walk in a way that silences the bell. When this happens, substitute a transistor radio for the bell.

2. Feed the cats. The cats may be killing and eating birds because they're hungry. Look closely at your neighbors' houses. Do they need to be painted? Are the lawns in bad shape? Your

neighbors may be too cheap to buy catfood for their pets. As far as your neighbors are concerned, they let the cats out and—by magic—the cats are fed! If you can, sculpt the catfood into the shape of a starling or pigeon.

3. Talk with the cats. Explain to them about birds, bees, and irate birders. People talk to cats all the time and the cats seem to understand, although they may not agree.

4. Buy a doberman.

5. Frequently loud noises work. Of course loud noises scare away birds, but birds come back quickly. Cats are a little more rational about sound. Some favorite noises are Led Zeppelin albums, a tape recording of a cat having its tail stepped on, and a sonic boom.

6. Scare the living daylights out of them. One man wrote to the *Dick E. Bird News* that he put his feeder on top of his car and hid inside. When a cat jumped on the hood he revved the engine, blasted the horn, and hit the brights. That cat has never been back.

7. Dig moats. Cats respect that.

8. Use high power water guns, especially the battery-operated type. This is Dick E. Bird's favorite anti-cat technique. He claims it is extraordinarily effective; after a few shots cats find other yards.

9. Buy mice and release them in your neighbor's yard. Cats prefer mice to birds because mice stay on the ground all the time, while birds force cats to try to fly.

10

Resources

 Bird and Outdoor Publications

The Dick E. Bird News
P.O. Box 377
Acme, MI 49610
Subscription price: $12 a year

The *Dick E. Bird News* is subtitled "The Best Darn BirdStories Ever Told." And that's what it is. The *Dick E. Bird News* is a monthly eight page tabloid that contains useful and fun information about the bird world. In it you'll not only learn how to attract birds, how to keep pests away from your feeder, how to take pictures of birds, ("You can't go through the woods like General Patton and hope to come out with an enjoyable experience, let alone a few good pictures"), but you'll find out about strange laws, such as the New Jersey law "making firecrackers legal by permit for the purpose of scaring birds away from cornfields," and the Connecticut statute that makes it a crime punishable by fine or imprisonment for "enticing of a neighbor's birds." The *Dick E. Bird News* is filled with photographs and drawings.

WildBird
Subscription Department
P.O. Box 6040
Mission Veijo, CA 92690-9983
Subscription price: 6 issues (one year) is $8.99

WildBird Magazine is a bimonthly four-color magazine. Typical articles include "Bargain Binoculars—Are They Good Enough For Birding?" "Sapsucker Woods—New York's Best-Known Birding Secret," and "Eastern Bluebirds—Back From the Brink." *WildBird* is best know for its color photographs. Each issue covers several features: field tests of outdoor birding equipment, tips taking pictures of birds, lists of birding events (free to outdoor organizations), and a species profile.

Bird Watcher's Digest
P.O. Box 110
Marietta, OH 45750
Subscription price: $15 a year

Bird Watcher's Digest, a bimonthly magazine, is the oldest and most popular birding magazine. Its *Reader's Digest* form makes it easy to take along on trips. And it's comprehensive. Anything you want to know about birds will be in *Bird Watcher's Digest.* A typical issue contained the following features: "Feeding Wild Turkeys," "Feeding the Birds," "Snow Geese at Brigantine," "FDR: Bird Watcher," and more. There's also verse and short fiction. The journal's regular departments include "The Behavior Watcher's Notebook," "Letters," book reviews, bird puzzles, and "The Backyard Bird Watcher's Question Box." The latter is one of *BWD*'s most valuable features—it's where readers can receive answers to their questions about birding. Because *BWD* has the largest number of readers of any bird magazine, it also has the most display and classified advertisements, which are frequently the best way to find out about new products and birding adventures. Each issue is filled with color and black and white photographs.

Birder's World
Subscription Department
P.O. Box 1347
Elmhurst, IL 60126-8347
Subscription: $25 a year

Birder's World, "The Magazine for Bird Enthusiasts," is a relative newcomer in the bird-magazine department. It's a bi-monthly, four color magazine that runs between 60 and 70 pages an issue. Typical articles include "To the Brink and Back: The Remarkable Comeback of the Wild Turkey," "Birds of the Pribilofs," and "Attracting Birds: Water, an Alluring Necessity." Each issue contains a bird art calendar, letters, book reviews, and photographs submitted by readers. The photographs in *Birder's World* are striking.

WingTips
Box 226
Lansing, NY 14882
Subscription: $10 a year

Wingtips is a small magazine that straddles the line between academic journal and popular magazine. The articles are informative and detailed, and you're likely to find information that's not available elsewhere. Current research in ornithology, notes about bird behavior, and meeting announcements are regularly featured in *WingTips*.

Bird Talk
Audubon Workshop
1501 Paddock Drive
Northbrook, IL 60062
Membership/subscription fee: $15/year

Bird Talk is a bimonthly newsletter published by the Audubon Workshop for the members of its Helping Hand Bird Club. The Audubon Workshop is a mail-order bird supply company, and the Helping Hand Bird Club provides discounts and other services to its members. This four-page newsletter contains well-researched articles about particular birds, how to attract birds, birds and acid rain, bird nests, and other topics.

The Bird Watch
Kansas State University
Manhattan, KS 66506

Subscription: $5 a year (regular), $10 a year family

The *Bird Watch* is a non-profit publication of the Bird Populations Institute. It is published 10 times a year and contains articles about bird feeding, bird habits, and answers to birding questions.

The Potomac Flier
Fairfax Audubon Society
P.O. Box 82
Vienna, VA 22180-8310

Subscription: $10 a year for non-members, free to members.

The *Potomac Flier* is published eight times a year by the Fairfax Audubon Society, part of the National Audubon Society. The eight page newsletter contains articles about local events, bird migrations, new books, seabirds, and Audubon Society activities.

Audubon Naturalist News
Audubon Naturalist Society
8940 Jones Mill Road
Chevy Chase, MD 20815

Subscription: Free to members. Membership is $20 for an individual, $28 for a family.

Published ten times a year by the Audubon Naturalist Society of the Central Atlantic States, the Audubon *Naturalist News* features articles about conservation, bird tours, and book reviews. The *News* comes in tabloid form and usually runs eight pages.

Wild Bird News
7687 MacArthur Blvd.
Cabin John, MD 20818

Subscriptions are free.

Published by the Wild Bird Center, which is located outside of Washington, D.C. along the Potomac River, *Wild Bird News* is one of the most interesting newsletters. It's published four to six times a year, and contains both articles about birding in the Washington area, and features about birds in general. One of *Wild Bird News'* most interesting features is "Ask George," in which publisher George Petrides answers questions about birding.

Sierra
730 Polk Street
San Francisco, CA 94190

Subscriptions are free to Sierra Club members. Membership is $33 a year for an individual membership, and $50 a year for a contributing membership.

Although not a birding magazine, *Sierra* frequently contains articles about birds and birding expeditions. *Sierra* is among the premier outdoor and conservation magazines. Its photographs are spectacular. In addition to its regular features, *Sierra* regularly publishes articles about nuclear waste, recycling, Congress and the environment, outdoor books, and travel spots. Several times a year the magazine lists Sierra Club trips.

Stores and Catalogs

Below are listed companies that sell wild bird supplies. Call or write these companies for their catalog or to order specific products.

Duncraft
Penacook, NH 03303
603-224-0200

Audubon Workshop
1501 Paddock Drive
Northbrook, IL 60062
312-729-6660

Wild Bird Center
7687 MacArthur Blvd.
Cabin John, MD 20818
301-229-3141

Noel's Bird Feeders
Northwood, NH 03261
603-942-8390

The Bird House
50 SW 2nd, Mezzanine
Portland, OR 97204
503-227-3232

Hyde Bird Feeder Company
56 Felton Street P.O. Box 168
Waltham, MA 02254

Droll Yankee Bird Feeders
Mill Road
Foster, RI 02825

Wild Bird Company
617 Hungerford Drive
Rockville, MD 20850
301-279-0079

Audubon Naturalist Society
8940 Jones Mill Road
Chevy Chase, MD 20815
301-652-3606

Stokes Nature Company
52 Nowell Farm Road
Carlisle, MA 01741

Bird Watcher's Digest Store
Box 110
Marierra, OH 45750

Natural History Books, Inc.
Box 1089
Lake Helen, FL 32744-1089

Quail, Inc.
Box 314
Thief River Falls, MN 56701

Nixalite of America
1025 16th Avenue
P.O. Box 727
East Moline, IL 61244
309-755-8771

The Bluebird House
9865 Lautenschlager Road
Apple Creek, OH 44606

Mr. Birdhouse
2307E Highway 2 West
Grand Rapids, MN 55744

Bird Houses & Supplies
21264 E. Via Verde
Covina, CA 91724

The Plow & Hearth
560 Main Street
Madison, VA 22727

The Barn Owl Gift Shop
2509 Lakeshore Drive
Fennville, MI 49408
616-543-4175

Princess Anne Farmers' Service
5651 Va. Beach Blvd.
Norfolk, VA 23502
804-461-1580

Wild Wings
Lake City, MN 55041
612-345-5355

McKinzie Scientific   Lancaster, OH 43130
1340 Kerr Avenue   614-687-4617
P.O. Box 1077
McKenzie Scientific specializes in wildlife damage control products. The company sells traps for relocating squirrels.

Further Reading

America's Favorite Backyard Birds, Kit and George Harrison, Simon and Schuster, 1983

The Bird Feeder Book, Donald and Lillian Stokes, Little Brown, 1987

How to Attract Birds, Ortho Books, 1983

The Natural History of Squirrels, John Gurnell, Facts on File, 1987

The Biology of Ground-Dwelling Squirrels, Jan O. Murie and Gail Michener, eds, University of Nebraska Press, 1984

Building Birdhouses and Bird Feeders, Ed and Stevie Baldwin, Doubleday, 1985

The Backyard Bird Watcher, George Harrison, Simon and Schuster, 1979

About the Author

Bill Adler, Jr. is a writer and book packager living in Washington, D.C. Adler is the president of Washington Independent Writers. He is the author of over half a dozen books including *The Wit and Wisdom of Wall Street* (Dow-Jones Books, 1984), *The Lottery Book* (William Morrow and Company, 1986) and *The Student's Memory Book* (Doubleday, 1988.) He is currently writing a novel about scotch whiskey. Adler lies awake at night, fearful that hordes of squirrels are massing to attack his house. He hopes that *Outwitting Squirrels* won't be his last book.